Infinite and Beyond
Deep Purple
1993-2022

Adrian Jarvis

Infinite and Beyond
Deep Purple
1993-2022

Adrian Jarvis

WYMER PUBLISHING
Bedford, England

First published in 2023 by Wymer Publishing
Bedford, England www.wymerpublishing.co.uk Tel: 01234 326691
Wymer Publishing is a trading name of Wymer (UK) Ltd

Copyright © 2023 Adrian Jarvis / Wymer Publishing.

Print edition (fully illustrated): **ISBN: 978-1-915246-38-7**

Edited by Jerry Bloom.

The Author hereby asserts his rights to be identified
as the author of this work in accordance with sections
77 to 78 of the Copyright, Designs & Patents Act 1988.

All rights reserved. No part of this publication may be
reproduced or transmitted in any form or by any means,
electronic or mechanical, including photocopying, or any
information storage and retrieval system, without written
permission from the publisher.

This publication is sold subject to the condition that it shall not,
by way of trade or otherwise, be lent, re-sold, hired out or
otherwise circulated without the publishers' prior consent in any
form of binding or cover other than that in which it is published
and without a similar condition including this condition
being imposed on the subsequent purchaser.

eBook formatting by Coinlea.
Printed and bound in Great Britain by
CMP, Dorset.

A catalogue record for this book is available from the British Library.

Typeset by Andy Bishop / Tusseheia Creative
Cover design by Tusseheia Creative

Contents

	Prologue: The Banjo Player Takes A Hike	7
1	From A Dreg To Royalty	17
2	On The Lonely Road	29
3	A Band On	37
4	A Load Of Orchestras	49
5	No Sleep 'til The Exit Door	63
6	Going Bananas	73
7	Enraptured	85
8	To Russia With Rock	97
9	One Eye To The Desert	105
10	Strings Attached	113
11	How Can I See When The Light Has Gone Out?	123
12	What Now?!	131
13	Sunflowers & Jam	143
14	Inducted	153
15	The Infinite Goodbye	163
16	Man (Still) Alive	171
17	Locked Down And Out	181
	Epilogue: After Time Ended	*193*
	Discography	*197*
	Filmography	*202*
	Endnotes	*203*

Prologue:
The Banjo Player Takes A Hike

The musicians assembled to the adoration of the crowd. Jon Lord took up position at his sheer stack of keyboards, Ian Paice ensconced himself behind his drum kit, Roger Glover picked up his bass guitar. Ian Gillan strode on to the stage, waving, acknowledging the whoops and whistles. Paice started an unmistakable machine gun beat, low at first, but gaining in intensity as the bass line kicked in, throbbing, expectant, as though waiting for something to happen. Then the Hammond organ arrived, building the sound, a chug, a grind, the introduction to the greatest opening song ever, Deep Purple's 'Highway Star'. Sweaty, heavy — and incomplete.

It went on. And on. Bewildered looks were exchanged on stage. Where was Ritchie Blackmore? Where was the guitar maestro whose fuzzbox-distorted Fender Stratocaster was supposed to take up the challenge and resolve everything in two crashing chords that explode into the verses?

He was nowhere to be seen.

Eventually, with a shrug, Gillan seemed to suggest that they get going anyway and a guitar-free version of the song blasted out from the stage over the increasingly bemused audience. It was not as bad as it could have been: Jon Lord proved equal to providing a passable approximation of the guitar parts, but that was just for this song. How would he do riff-driven classics such as 'Smoke on the Water'? Two verses in and a major crisis was looming. The guitar solo was coming up — how would they fudge that?

The second chorus over, Blackmore finally appeared, ambling on to the stage, picking at his strings. Gillan gave a sweeping gesture, more of relief than welcome, and the band continued as a five piece. From the audience, it was easy to believe that it had all been a deliberate thing, a coup de theatre. Sadly not, because it was not over yet.

Blackmore completed the solo, crossed the stage, grabbed a plastic glass full of water and threw it over someone. This hapless individual was later revealed to be one of the cameramen recording the event for a video release called, appropriately, *Come Hell or High Water*.

It was an inauspicious start to a gig that Gillan, in his autobiography, described, a little unfairly, as Deep Purple's worst ever[1]. It was also the culmination of a problem that had long been building up to an eruption. The cameraman was simply collateral damage. The place was the NEC Arena in Birmingham, the date was November 9th 1993, but the arm that threw the glass had been priming itself for the previous nine years — and perhaps for even longer than that.

To understand what happened, it is necessary to go back to the early seventies, when — according to Lord — Gillan and Blackmore, 'agreed to disagree.'[2] At that time, the classic Mark II line-up — the one that appeared at the NEC on that notorious night — was flying high, but outward appearances can be deceiving. Unable to take the pressure anymore, Gillan quit, which led, at Blackmore's behest, to the sacking of Glover and the construction of what was effectively a new band that just happened to share the name of the old one — with Mark III added.

Soon enough, the whole creaky enterprise fizzled out and, in 1976, Deep Purple split. Blackmore had already started a band called Rainbow that was surprisingly excellent for most of its life and included Glover in its line-up for many of its albums. Gillan went on to the modestly-monikered Ian Gillan

Band, which morphed into the equally self-effacing Gillan. Lord and Paice — arguably the best musicians of all — ended up as journeymen, playing in Whitesnake, a band put together by Mark III alumnus, David Coverdale: this lot produced whole albums filled with songs about Coverdale's cock.

Throughout the eight-year period during which Deep Purple were on 'hiatus', rumours of a reunion never went away, even as the likelihood of it happening receded more and more into the distance. Then, quite suddenly, in 1984, it happened.

They said that it was all about the music, although Blackmore later conceded that they were not being strictly truthful.[3] The various hiatus projects were doing well enough, but no one was getting all that rich off the back of them. Lord and Paice, in particular, were paycheque players: they needed little goading to drop what they were doing and sign up. Glover had some misgivings, but was open to persuasion and Blackmore involved himself with alacrity, albeit because, as he has said, 'The manager called me up and said that there was a lot of money in this.'[4]

Gillan was bullish about it all at the time, but later admitted that there was much nervousness and more than a few doubts ahead of everyone's first meeting. He had recently made a rather unwise commitment to front Purple's contemporaries, Black Sabbath, which seems to have been an unhappy experience all round. He has said that he was 'disgusted' by the one album that was produced, the less-than-classic *Born Again*.[5] Perhaps he was pleased to be given an escape route that no one would question as insincere or contrived.

Revived Deep Purple certainly had to include all five. Mark II could command whatever fees they wanted. Eighty percent of the band with a different singer would have convinced nobody (it would not be long before that possibility was tested out — with predictable results).

Rapprochements effected, the band reassembled, signed to

Polygram for an allegedly sizable advance[6] and released *Perfect Strangers*, a good, if not outstanding, return that made a big dent in the charts, but, more importantly, provided the impetus for a number of lucrative tours.

It seemed that bygones could indeed be bygones. For a while. Live recordings from this period (mostly released a long time after the event) showcase a band on top form and, as far as could be discerned, enjoying being back together. Three years passed in such activity before the next studio-based material emerged, in the form of the distinctly underwhelming *The House of Blue Light*.

Of this one, Lord said: '[It] was a weird album and hard to put together. We made the massive mistake of trying to make our music current. We discovered that people didn't want us to do that. They wanted us to do what we do best. We're Deep Purple — loud, proud, pure and simple.'[7] It was the first indication that old problems were beginning to rise once again to the surface.

The House of Blue Light was quickly followed by a disastrous live effort, *Nobody's Perfect*. Intended to be the successor to the band's legendary *Made in Japan*, it was launched with much (strangely) Medieval fanfare.[8] It pleased precisely no one. The fact that it featured much unnecessary editing and that bête noire of the live album fan, overdubs, has often been seen as a reason for its failure. That it was filled with *The House of Blue Light* songs of ephemeral appeal might also be mentioned.

Polygram were getting jittery as it was becoming increasingly obvious that their investment was not paying off. *Nobody's Perfect* received such bad press that it began to affect ticket sales. Hitherto healthy, they tanked to the extent that in 1988 an entire North American tour was cut back to a single gig. In the background, band dynamics were also going in the wrong direction. Gillan and Blackmore were again, at best, in a state of non-communication.

Matters came to a head in 1989, when sessions for a proposed new album spilled over into major arguments, primarily over musical direction. Blackmore was keen on a poppier, more melodic approach, similar to that adopted by the later versions of Rainbow. The singer wanted to create something grand and heavy on production values. He did not get his way and, at the instigation of Blackmore, was fired.

On the guitarist's recommendation, ex-Rainbow vocalist Joe Lynn Turner was drafted in as a replacement. This version of Deep Purple — little more than Rainbow redux with Paice and Lord once again relegated to second banana status — produced an album, *Slaves and Masters*, that was emphatically not a crowd-pleaser.

Its title has certainly not aged well (in fact, it rather innocently refers to parts of the recording process), but it is not actually as bad as many fans would wish to believe. For sure, the cover is awful. Inspired by the track 'Fortuneteller', it is a children's book illustration that is gaudy and inappropriate for a band of Deep Purple's sensibilities.

Most of the songs, to be fair, are pretty good in their own right, but they are light rock, MOR, not the pounding heavy insanity for which Purple are renowned. A massive negative is that the track listing includes what is probably Deep Purple's worst ever effort, 'Love Conquers All,' a monstrosity so bad that it even elicited some uncharacteristic negativity from Jon Lord: 'There was this beautiful piece, which Ritchie and I had written, 'Love Conquers All.' We once played it late at night, that is Ritchie and I played it together. It was very sad, very melancholy, it was introspective, but it was absolutely a Purple song, a bit like 'When A Blind Man Cries' or the quiet parts in 'Child In Time' or 'Wasted Sunsets' — a ballad of the kind we sometimes play, a blues ballad. But then Joe appeared and turned it into some sort of cabaret song.'[9]

No official live releases have ever been made available from this mark of the band, but a few pirated films can be seen on YouTube. They do not make for happy viewing. On the plus side, the set list was able to expand to take in songs from marks that did not include Gillan. But that does little to disguise how wrong Turner was at the front. Where strutting arrogance and macho posturing are required, he could only bounce around like an auditioning holiday camp entertainer, doing what Blackmore described as 'little twee movements.'[10]

Turner worked hard to bring every member of the audience into the show, but he had no chemistry with his fellow performers. They played with their heads down in a joyless display that is a far cry from the excitement of a Gillan-led gig. More serious was Turner's voice. He is a great singer, that cannot be denied, but he is a great singer of pop and the frothier bits of rock. He is simply out of his depth with the Deep Purple repertoire.

While this was all going on, a significant year was coming ever closer, 1993 — Deep Purple's twenty fifth anniversary. The prospect of reaching this milestone with Turner was not an appetising one to the record company and at least three members of the band. The fourth, Blackmore, made a show of resistance, but accepted the inevitable. Turner was unceremoniously shown the door. Efforts now turned to getting Gillan back.

This was easier said than done. Not only had his sacking been the culmination of his long rivalry with Blackmore, but he had also publicly declared that he would rather have his throat cut than play with Deep Purple again.[11] He had, moreover, resumed his solo career, racking up reasonable sales with the album *Naked Thunder*, although not so much with its follow-up, *Toolbox*. Notwithstanding this, his old mate Glover worked on him over a period of time and he agreed to eat his words and rejoin.

It was not to be a glorious comeback. The anniversary

album, *The Battle Rages On...* — apt as its title is — was a huge disappointment. Most of the songs had already been written before Gillan's return — with Turner in mind as their singer. Gillan contributed some new lyrics and a few new melodies, but he was all too aware that he was not much more than a session player, interpreting someone else's material. The finished album is competent, but very ordinary and unmemorable. It was a poor way to mark a major moment in the band's career. Still, the band diligently, if perfunctorily, took it on tour.

It would be nice to be able to report that this went well, but the antagonism between singer and guitarist flared up again. Relations became so strained that the two even started to take different routes on to the stage in order to avoid having to bump into each other. Blackmore, tiring of what he saw as a lack of professionalism on Gillan's part, tendered his resignation, agreeing only to complete the European leg. He felt driven to do this by the epiphany that sacking Gillan would never be enough — the singer would always come back, like a long-haired terminator. The only way to guarantee a distance from him was for Blackmore to go. He arrived in Birmingham on November 9th effectively on notice.

The thrown water went close to Gillan, who was boosting the solo with a turn on the congas, but Blackmore maintained that it was not aimed at his bandmate: 'I was told by my management at the time that BMG [the band's label] wanted to film the show at the NEC. I agreed to this providing there would be no cameramen on the side of the stage. I find they put me off my performance.'[12] The promise of no camera operators apparently having been reneged upon put Blackmore into a mood that constrained his entire performance.

Afterwards, news of his imminent departure leaked out and the last few shows — culminating in Helsinki — were sullen, low key, affairs that those involved would probably prefer to forget. It should be mentioned that there was no repetition of the water-throwing incident — or anything like it.

Somewhat presumptuously, Blackmore saw this as, de facto, the end for the band as a whole. He informed management and promoters that planned gigs in Japan were cancelled. His was not an opinion shared by his colleagues. They were keen to bring in a new guitarist and carry on.

In terms of where this story is heading, this is a major plot point. In the minds of many, Deep Purple the brand was synonymous with the people who comprised it. Specifically, it was not distinct from the Mark II line-up. Blackmore was acting on this assumption when he called off the remaining gigs: since he was Deep Purple, it could not continue without him. But that is never how it was.

The Gillan-fronted band may have been the most famous and successful, but it was still only Mark II — there had been a Mark I before it. It was also not unprecedented for the band to work with a different guitarist. Blackmore had first quit in 1975, to be replaced, for one superb album, by Tommy Bolin. It was true that this was something of an aberration and that Blackmore had been the driving force of almost everything else that the band had done, but he was reckoning without the pragmatism of his colleagues. They were professionals, after all, and the one thing that professionals know is that the show must go on!

Blackmore resurrected the corpse of Rainbow for an album *Stranger In Us All* that was a good listen, but still a rehash of a rehash of a rehash. Deep Purple meanwhile needed someone to take on six-string duties — and quickly. They approached the successful solo artist Joe Satriani, who said 'no' on the grounds that he was a massive fan of Blackmore and couldn't see how he could possibly replace him. He changed his mind within half an hour, describing the offer as, 'One of those ideas where you have to think about it for a bit. And you go, "Yeah, this is totally outside the box, but maybe it's a way to keep celebrating the legacy, and maybe I'll learn something.'"¹³

With only two weeks' preparation time, Satriani joined and the Japanese shows were a triumph. Glover later said, 'We had so much fun doing those six gigs. What a revelation!'¹⁴ Such sentiments would have been inconceivable just weeks earlier.

Again, official releases of live material from this period have remained, sadly, unforthcoming. Grainy films of concerts on YouTube confirm what Glover was saying. Satriani knocks out the riffs as though he was born playing them (maybe he was) and makes solos his own. As Glover noted, if Blackmore's departure left a question mark as to whether audiences would accept a new guitarist, the answer was a resounding 'yes'. Everybody was having such a good time that Satriani stuck around for European dates in 1994.

Now, though, the bigger picture had to be considered. Satriani had done sterling work as a temporary stand-in, but there would be more tours in the future and, at some point, new recorded material. Would he agree to staying for a bit longer? Would he become a permanent member of the band? In a recent interview, he explained why he decided against this, 'I just thought, I'm Joe from Long Island. I don't belong in this British royalty metal band. I knew I just didn't belong. I was a big fan of Ritchie Blackmore and I thought I'll never be able to rectify it. I'll always feel guilty that I have to copy Ritchie and I didn't want to do that.'¹⁵

He already enjoyed a successful and highly respected solo career that he had not built overnight. To abandon it would have been to throw a lot of work and time and tears in the trash. Besides, as he realised, to step into the shoes of a famous and much-loved predecessor would have been to consign himself to a lifetime of being compared to that person, usually — however unfairly — unfavourably. This proved to be all too prescient as far as Blackmore's eventual permanent successor was concerned.

All agreed that the Joe Satriani brand of Deep Purple had been a glorious experiment, but the planets had not been sufficiently well aligned for it to become anything more. Still, the band were rejuvenated. The dreadful time that all had endured during the *The Battle Rages On…* days was over. The misery was gone. But that did leave the band facing one not insignificant problem. If they were to continue, Blackmore had to be replaced. To borrow Gillan's perhaps unwittingly disparaging phrase, they needed a new banjo player…

1
From A Dreg To Royalty

A fast, heavy guitar chug starts the track. It sounds metallic, like some tuned-to-the-max engine starting up. Then huge chords, like stabs of brass, enter and begin to bash out a tune. Their power is resolved by a slowing down as the guitar, now high-pitched and full of longing, noodles around, bringing everything back to its starting point. More of those power chords, more soloing guitar and an ever-increasing pitch. It sounds like it should be finished, resolved, but it has only just begun. A drum solo, then a call-and-response guitar and drum section. Then — more of it: hard, fast, heavy. Solos, including a guitar run that takes in the treble and bass strings, rockabilly-style.

The track is the instrumental, 'Take It Off The Top' by The Dixie Dregs. Many English rock fans of a certain age (your humble author included) will immediately recognise it as the theme tune to Tommy Vance's legendary *Friday Rock Show*, a weekly date with the radio that was virtually a distance-learning night school for devotees of fuzzbox-infused music.

The most important element of the tune for the purposes of this story is the identity of the guitarist, Steve Morse. Anyone listening to that track can be in no doubt of one thing — that Morse is prodigiously talented. He is easily the equal of Blackmore — in that respect, at least. The conductor Paul Mann, with whom Morse would go on to work extensively, said of him: 'He was born with that instrument in his hands. I know a lot of classical musicians who envy that kind of relationship with an instrument: to have no barrier between your head and your fingers and your heart and your fingers.'[1]

Morse was born in Hamilton, Ohio on 28th July 1954, although he also lived as a young man in Tennessee (hence, perhaps, the 'Dixie' element of the Dregs) and Michigan. These simple biographical facts immediately distinguish him from the members of Deep Purple. For a start, he was younger than they were. Ian Paice was the 'baby' of the band, and he had been born in 1948. Jon Lord, having entered the world in 1941, was almost a whole other generation. These age gaps may not seem large — after all, the difference between Paice and Lord was greater than that between Paice and Morse, but, culturally, they were significant. Morse missed out on the 1960s in a way that Deep Purple's members did not and, in order to fully understand Deep Purple, they need to be placed into the context of the sixties.[2]

Equally significant was Morse's American nationality. Deep Purple had welcomed in American members before, Joe Lynn Turner and Joe Satriani most recently. In both of these cases, the impact on the band's identity was less profound than it could have been. The former had been intended as a permanent member, but had obviously not fitted in, while the latter was effectively a zero-hours-contract roadie.

A better analogy for Morse would be Tommy Bolin. The so-called Mark IV line-up's one album, *Come Taste The Band*, has come to be acknowledged as a classic, but was dismissed at the time. Its blatant funk influences caused considerable bemusement to a fan base that only really wanted another Mark II. Even Jon Lord described it as 'not a Deep Purple album,'[3] a position he maintained for the rest of his life. 'Take It Off The Top' is a fun, raucous, exciting piece of music, but, like *Come Taste the Band*, it does not sound much like classic Deep Purple.

In other ways, too, Morse seems like an odd match for Purple. He is college-educated, having attended the University of Miami School of Music. While there, he formed his first major band, the creatively-named Rock Ensemble II. This distinguishes him from almost all the members of Deep Purple, who, typical of working-class English people of their vintage, finished their formal educations early. Jon Lord was the sole exception; in that he earned a diploma in acting.

His higher education complete, Morse started Dixie Dregs with fellow alumnus Andy West. Despite sounding like a gang of dungaree-wearing shitkickers, the Dregs played a sophisticated type of fusion rock. Listening to Morse's own account of the writing of 'Take It Off The Top' underlines this point: 'It started out really rock — my love of Jimmy Page and Jeff Beck — but I began to add a bunch of contrapuntal elements to the bridge. My jazz side was coming through'[4].

Signed first by Capricorn Records and, later, by Arista, the Dregs released a series of albums (with tracks mostly written by Morse) that garnered good reviews, but poor sales. Nonetheless, Morse steadily gained an individual reputation and following. His compositions on the album *Industry Standard* led to its winning a prize from *Guitar Player*, while Morse himself began a five-year reign as the magazine's 'Best Overall Guitarist'. Producer Ken Scott, who worked with Morse on various projects, rated him best guitarist, period, saying, 'He covers all styles, from classical, acoustic — there's one track on one of the albums called 'Little Kids' which is him and just solo violin, which is brilliant.'[5]

The Dixie Dregs folded in 1983 and Morse — sort of — went solo, forming The Steve Morse Band, a power trio. For a while, he moved backwards and forwards between projects, joining Kansas in 1986 for two albums, before reforming his own band and even going back to a resuscitated Dregs in the late eighties. This restlessness was to continue even after he found a longer-term day job, as he lent his talents to a bewildering array of side projects, tours and guest slots. For a couple of years, he even worked as a commercial airline pilot — something that happens with rock musicians more often than seems attributable to pure chance.[6]

What it all added up to was an impressive CV that made him a 'musicians' musician' without forcing him to the front of the public's consciousness as a bona fide axe hero. That was to come next, when a certain band sat down to decide who should be a permanent replacement for their recently departed guitarist. The story goes that each of Deep Purple's members made a shortlist of their preferred candidates, every one having the same name at the top: Steve Morse.[7] This is a lovely story that there is no reason to disbelieve, but it seems a little too convenient — designed more to demonstrate solidarity than to be an accurate reflection of reality.

Whatever the truth, Morse was approached and asked what he thought about coming aboard. The initial conversations were cagey on both sides. For his part, Morse was uncertain as to whether he would fit in: 'I wanted [a trial period] because Purple never toured much in the US… so when my manager called me about it, I said, "I don't know, it all depends on the band, you know." He said, "it's Deep Purple." I said, "yeah, but what are the people like? What is the music like? And can they still play, you know?" It's a lot of question marks, you know — I don't want to go out there and be a nostalgia act.'[8]

At the time, Morse's main worry, strangely, was that he might be forced to accept a dress code. As he explained, though, he was less worried about having to wear a costume like a member of some latter-day Kiss, than musical compatibility, 'I'd never seen them live, so my question wasn't so much about dressing, but the point was do they know what I do, do they have any idea that I'm different than what some audience members might expect of a Ritchie Blackmore replacement.'[9]

The days when Tommy Bolin complained about having to replicate Blackmore's style note for note were long over. Glover's take was, 'When we were looking for a guitarist before Steve, I remember mentioning the fact that, "Yeah, we can get a young kid guitarist and he has all the right looks and everything like that but it's got to be a virtuoso. It's got to be someone who is really different and special." And Steve Morse fitted that bill. He is different and special. I remember him asking me, "What do you want from me?" and I said, "I want you to be 100% yourself." You're not replacing Ritchie Blackmore.'[10]

Suitably reassured, Morse met Roger Glover at a club called Ziggy's in Winston-Salem, North Carolina. While there, the two had a picture taken that, with the other members of the band photoshopped in, would go on to become the first publicity shot for the new line-up.

Social compatibility established, the musical personalities still needed to gel, so, as Morse put it: 'We did a little trial period and after the first, I'd say, hour, everyone was smiling, and we had instant communication. Like I'd play stuff and Jon would be, oh yeah, how about this? He had taken what I was doing and transposed it or added a harmony on to it or something like that and I'd go, whoa, how did you do that? And Roger and Ian Paice, their playing… they were like one of those bands that had the feeling.'[11]

Three days of rehearsals in Mexico City preceded Morse's first appearance with Deep Purple, which took place on November 23rd 1994 — almost exactly one year after the NEC debacle. The set list[12] was not very different from that which the band had played during the dying days of the Blackmore era — some oldies, mostly lifted from their biggest selling album, *Machine Head*, and a few of the more concert-friendly numbers from *The Battle Rages On*....

That said, some of the experimentation that would become a feature of the so-called 'Morse era' was evident even then. For a start, the bluesy ballad, 'When A Blindman Cries', originally brought in during Satriani's tenure, made an appearance. Recorded as part of the *Machine Head* sessions, it is one of the band's best songs, but was relegated to B-side ignominy at the behest of Blackmore, who disliked it.[13]

Its long overdue rehabilitation came when a remastered version of the album was released in 1997, on which it took its rightful place among the other songs. It was not the only moment of novelty that marked Morse's debut.

The title track to Mark II's second studio album, *Fireball*, got an airing, too. As close as Deep Purple have ever come to thrash metal, this bonkers foray into discordant excess was played live a couple of times in the early seventies but had remained unperformed ever since. So successful was its second chance that it soon became a set opener. The enjoyable *Machine Head* also-ran 'Pictures Of Home' was similarly dragged out of retirement to shine once more.

Not surprisingly, there was no new material. That would appear soon enough. For now, a couple of things were obvious. The first was that any fears that the band would never again reach the heights of live virtuosity scaled with their original guitarist were proven spectacularly misplaced.

The second was that audiences were quite prepared to accept Morse largely without prejudice. This is not to say that everyone was convinced, but he was far from a flop — indeed, in future years, the band with him in a central role would achieve successes (by some measures) the like of which they had not matched since, *Perfect Strangers*.

The tour continued with dates in, among others places, Monterey, California and Corpus Christi in Texas. More tinkering with the set list occurred, the country-flavoured 'Anyone's Daughter' — which had been performed at the NEC — making a comeback.

Things were working out very satisfactorily, but everyone was conscious that one reason for Satriani not being considered a 'proper' member of the band was that he had not appeared on any studio recordings: thoughts began to turn to a new album.

Nothing could be done, however, until Gillan had completed another commitment. He got back together with his old mates from the 1960s, The Javelins, to record an album, that was released in September. Consisting exclusively of covers, it made no real impact on the charts and was roundly ignored by Deep Purple fans. Indeed, it is now so obscure that an article about it on Wikipedia has a notice threatening deletion on the grounds that the subject lacks 'notability'. It is interesting, though, for a couple of reasons. One is the track listing, which, although mainly made up of rock 'n' roll standards, includes songs by the likes of Smokey Robinson — an indication of the eclecticism of Gillan's output that would become more evident as he moved into the new millennium.

Side projects by the members of Deep Purple had a long history. Back in the 1970s Mark II glory days, Blackmore and Paice, performing under pseudonyms, had taken part in an eccentric piece of work called *Green Bullfrog*, Gillan had sung on the original recording of *Jesus Christ Superstar*, Lord had begun a career as a classical composer, putting out *The Gemini Suite*, *Windows* and *Sarabande*, while Glover had been the driving force behind the concept album, *The Butterfly Ball*.

But these were rarities and certainly since the 1984 reformation, Deep Purple had been a demanding employer, leaving little time for solo work. That was not to be the case in the new era and non-band releases by Deep Purple's members would come to outnumber those by the band as a whole. Morse, who became a prolific moonlighter, was adamant that this was a good thing, 'I think it's absolutely a necessity [that members of the band engage in wider work]. With the band, out of necessity, you end up with a repetition when you are doing a tour and musicians can only stand so much repetition.'[14]

In February 1995, work began on the first Deep Purple album to feature Morse. Recordings took place at Greg Rike Productions in Altamonte Springs, Florida, and went on —

and off and on — until October. Concurrently, the band kept themselves busy touring, although there was a scaling down in ambition. America and Europe were more-or-less ignored, but audiences in South Africa were treated to ten concerts. To publicise them, Glover, Lord and Morse appeared on South African radio in March where they played an acoustic set comprised of instrumental versions of some of the band's songs, as well as a new tune called 'The Highland'. By the time lyrics were added it became 'The Aviator'.[15] The resulting recording is enough to make any Deep Purple aficionado yearn for the unplugged album that never was…

A show in Bombay on 8th April was filmed and released (and reissued later as part of a DVD box set.) Later still — much later: 2022, in fact — it came out as a live album. The set list is basically that which had been the standard since Gillan's return, with one exception: 'The Purpendicular Waltz' came fresh from recording sessions that were yet to yield a public output.

One finally hit the shops in February 1996 under the pre-spoilered title *Purpendicular*. Glover described the process of coming up with that as having a similar level of near supernatural serendipity as the recruitment of Morse: 'We had to get a name for the album very early and *Purpendicular* was the only serious contender and there was no — no one else said anything, so we said, "fine let's do it" and it was just so easy.'[16]

Unfortunately, as a pun, *Purpendicular* is not as witty as Glover seems to think it is. Blatantly influenced by Ozzy Osborne's almost contemporaneous *Ozzmosis*, it is one of several ways in which the album makes an underwhelming initial impression. The cover, too (bafflingly based on a sketch of a breaking match against a blank purple background) looks like it took all of ten minutes to knock up.

Fortunately, fans were not so superficial and digging deeper reveals a host of riches. What struck many immediately were the credits: for the first time since the early seventies, all of the songs were credited to all of the band. Presumably, again, the intention was to emphasise that Morse was not a replacement or stand-in, but legitimately Blackmore's anointed successor.

Glover, in an interview from March 1996, gives another reason for the move back to democracy: 'Steve's contribution to the writing process was just wonderful and crucial. Not just because of his ideas and his playing but because of the positive attitude that he brought to it. One of the bugbears over the years, since 1973 in fact, has been publishing, writing credits, who writes what, who gets what. It's been like a shadow over the proceedings, that over time, had turned into an absolute storm. It kills the creative process.'[17]

Musically, the album is outstanding, far better than anyone still reeling from the *The Battle Rages On…* nightmare had any right to expect. As a rule, a good way to gauge the level of Deep Purple's creativity is how clichéd, or not, are their song titles. The higher the level of cliché, the lower the level of creativity. *The Battle Rages On…* is a catalogue of clichés, filled, as it is, with songs called 'One Man's Meat', 'Nasty Piece Of Work', 'Time To Kill', 'Twist in the Tale'. Even the title track is not exactly original. The song titles for *Purpendicular*, by contrast, are filled with originality, quirkiness and intrigue.

First up is 'Vavoom: Ted the Mechanic'. Ostensibly, a true story, this recounts a mundane conversation between a nameless narrator and the eponymous character at a strip club. Its lyrics are notable for including the previously referenced, if oblique, criticism of Blackmore in the line, 'The banjo player took a hike'. On first hearing, it is something of a jolt. Heavy and chugging, with pinched harmonics not heard before, it sounds sort-of like Deep Purple, but also not. There is no intricate riff, just a heavy beat. Even the bridge, when Morse heads up the frets to lighten everything up a bit, is not typical of the band. As an opening statement about new directions, it is rather stunning. Next up is the ballad 'Loosen My Strings', then the semi-dissonant 'Soon Forgotten' before acoustic guitars are broken out for parts of the lengthy 'Sometimes I Feel Like Screaming', the lyrics to which are autobiographical, a point about which Gillan has never been remotely coy.

Experimentation continues with the folky 'Aviator', the funky, moody, bass-led 'Rosa's Cantina' and the poppy 'A Touch Away'. A 'bonus' track, 'Don't Hold Your Breath' was made available in Japan, but has been hard to come by anywhere else (it can be heard on YouTube). This is just as well, since, for all of its invention and virtuosity, it is rather disjointed in structure, with almost completely melody-free verses.

Across the album, Morse is, as is to be expected, to the fore, Lord contenting himself with a supporting role (albeit one that makes him more integral to the sound than he is on *The Battle Rages On*....) That said, Gillan's parts are arguably more interesting. For a start, much of the singing adopts the 'talking blues' style that he introduced as early as 1971 on the *Fireball* album. Songs such as 'Ted the Mechanic' and 'Somebody Stole My Guitar' are as much rap as rock. There is a newfound and refreshing emphasis on storytelling — an antidote to the dreary assertions that passed for lyrics on the previous album.

The stories are often set in a somewhat fanciful version of America. Whether it is the Texan or Mexican deserts that provide the backdrops to 'Rosa's Cantina', 'Hey Cisco' and 'Somebody Stole My Guitar', the Hispanic stylings of 'Sometimes I Feel Like Screaming', or the blue-collar bar in which Ted and the narrator talk about everything except religion, American social, cultural and physical landscapes are ever present. It seems that a deliberate decision was taken to lean in to the nationality of the band's newest member — and the America described is not that of Manhattan sophisticates, Californian poseurs, or Harvard intellectuals, but one inhabited by, well, Dixie Dregs.

On the negative side, it must be admitted that, as an

example of album curation, *Purpendicular* leaves much to be desired. The heaviest — perhaps most typically Deep Purple — songs are all stuck at the end ('the end of side 2' in old money), meaning that a set that is otherwise wide ranging takes a turn towards metal right at the end in a way that makes the tracks in question — 'Hey Cisco', 'Somebody Stole My Guitar' and 'The Purpendicular Waltz' — seem somehow less important than those that precede them. Perhaps they are (although the first of this trio would become a concert staple for quite a while).

Perhaps the point was to demonstrate that this was a new brand of Purple. Yes, the history would be respected, but anything would be permitted in the name of creativity and fun. After all, the album can only loosely be described as heavy rock. It is a rock album, for sure, but only parts of it — arguably, the less exhilarating parts — are 'heavy.'

Purpendicular was released on 17th February 1996, three years — minus change — after *The Battle Rages On*....

2
On The Lonely Road

The album was not a runaway success. As of this writing, it has still sold only two thirds the number of copies of its unloved predecessor — and that had not had Michael Jackson looking nervously over his shoulder.[1] The only countries in which *Purpendicular* came out on top were Germany and Finland (although the margins were tight). It is probably just as well that Glover's attitude was to poo-poo the charts altogether: 'The thought of being 'commercial' on this album was never ever discussed. There was no thought of doing a radio friendly song or anything like that.'[2] He seems to have forgotten 'Loosen My Strings' and 'A Touch Away', both of which are about as radio-friendly as it is possible to get.

Looking at sales figures for the band's albums as a series, it is clear that *The Battle Rages On...* was the point at which things went alarmingly south.[3] Up until then, every release, including the much-maligned *Slaves And Masters* had shifted in excess of a million copies worldwide. *The Battle Rages On...* got close, but not close enough, and everything released since has fallen well short of the magic mark — despite sometimes appearing high up in various countries' charts. At the time of *Purpendicular*, this would have been due to Deep Purple's appeal becoming — to coin a phrase — more selective; these days, it probably better represents changing listening habits among fans.

Still, in an effort to drum up sales, the year 1996 was spent on the road, the band racking up an impressive quantity of gigs. To a large extent, it was a period of testing the market without leaving well-established comfort zones. Although the previous year had seen the band adding some rarely-if-ever-before-visited countries to the list of those that would comprise a 'world' tour, now the emphasis was on Europe, with a few dates in North America.

The tentativeness was further reflected in the venues that were booked. Whereas the 'Come Hell…' drama had played out in the cavernous interior of the NEC Arena, this time out, the Birmingham leg of the tour took place on 29th February in Aston Villa Leisure Centre — essentially a repurposed sports hall. It was, to say the least, a more intimate environment.

Whereas for most bands of any scale today — and, in more 'normal' times, Deep Purple — a 'national' tour of the UK would mean appearances at the five or six stadia large enough to accommodate them, the 1996 tour more closely resembled the on-the-road experience of the band at the very start of their career. They played many more gigs than they had become used to and found themselves criss-crossing the country as they headed from one small-to-medium-sized venue to another. Manchester Apollo one night, Liverpool Empire the next.

The pattern continued as they crossed the Channel to bring their act to Europe. A bewildering multiplicity of towns and cities was visited, often involving the leaving of a country, only to return to it a week or two later. By the time they reached the USA and Canada, they were a tight and extremely well-practised unit. Any doubts about Morse's capacity to fit in had long since ebbed away.

Such physical constraints seem to have freed the band in other, less tangible, ways. Presumably resigning themselves to life as a niche act playing to a shrinking, but dedicated, fan base, song selection no longer had to conform to Blackmore's narrow definition of acceptable. As a result, not only was *Purpendicular* very well represented, but the trend to involve rarities from the past was indulged in to the full. In Birmingham, they even played 'Rat Bat Blue' from the *Who Do We Think We Are* album: live performances of this one — never mind live recordings — are about as common as pictures of Gillan and Blackmore smiling at the same time.

A flavour of the sound being produced can be gained by listening to the release (bizarrely marketed as an 'official bootleg') *Live At The Olympia*, recorded in Paris on 17th June. Of the venue, the reader can be directed to the always-generous Internet to find out more about its legendary status among rock fans (one word: Hendrix).

Regarding the set list, no less than six of the seventeen songs played are from the new album. Some are obvious choices — 'Ted the Mechanic' (now with 'Vavoom' dropped), 'The Purpendicular Waltz', 'Hey Cisco' — others less so — 'Sometimes I Feel Like Screaming', 'Cascades: I'm Not Your Lover' and 'Rosa's Cantina'. All work surprisingly well in the live context, complementing more established material to good effect. Of that, the old *Machine Head* stagers are present and correct, but so is 'Fireball' and another, very funky, talking blues, song, 'No One Came'. The latter might be the boldest inclusion of the lot.

Missing is 'Child in Time', from the *In Rock* album. Long lauded as the band's masterpiece, it had been a concert mainstay since it was written in 1969 — at least for the Gillan-led versions of the band (the 'marks' that featured David Coverdale had their own equivalent in 'Mistreated'). Blackmore had pretty much insisted on its inclusion. It had always been something of a bugbear for Gillan.[4]

At the top end of his range, he struggled to reach all the notes and the screaming section — probably the most stunning part of the song — had placed considerable strains on his voice. Even at the height of his powers, he had been prone to ask that it be dropped from the set — a request that Blackmore had often gleefully denied, playing its introduction and thus presenting his rival with a fait accompli.

Now many years, a medical problem with his vocal chords[5] and plenty of cigarettes down the line, belting the song out night after night on a long tour was out of the question. It was, Gillan averred, a 'young man's song'[6] and, therefore, not one for him anymore. Apart from a couple of performances in the early 2000s, it has been off the menu since soon after Blackmore's departure.

Equally significant is the fact that the members of Deep Purple are not the only musicians present. On a number of tracks, they are joined by a small horn section, consisting of trumpet, saxophone and trombone. Quite what motivated their inclusion need not be gone into, but, as guest appearances go, it is extraordinarily happy. The horns are not especially prominent, but they can be heard boosting power chords and adding new dimensions to familiar riffs.

The band had involved other musicians before, of course, most memorably — and spectacularly — in Jon Lord's rock/classical crossover pieces from the late sixties and early seventies. Since then, they had eschewed working with anyone else. The average Deep Purple album achieves an astonishingly rich sonic palette, so, arguably, other people were simply not required. Even so, *Live At The Olympia* can be seen as the start of a trend in the direction of a more expansive attitude towards album and tour personnel that would carry on right up to what — at the time of writing — can be called the present day.

Perhaps the essence of Deep Purple in concert at this time (at least as released) comes with the album, *Live At Montreux 1996* (released in 2006). Part of a series of recorded performances by a wide range of artists from the Montreux Jazz Festival in Switzerland — which, in common with most 'Jazz Festivals' these days, has little to do with actual jazz — it features tracks from the band's appearance on 9th July, augmented with some from their later booking in 2000.

The band's history with the town of Montreux was long and especially close. As Mark II, they played at the Montreux Casino in 1969 for a gig that was so early in their career that some songs had not even reached their final form as yet. A recording of it was put out in the early 2000s as *Kneel and Pray*, that being the title given to the urtext of their classic 'Speed King' to which they treated the audience. Most poignantly, it was while they were recording *Machine Head* in Montreux that the events immortalised by 'Smoke on the Water' occurred. The band returned to the town to lay down their first album of the post-Gillan and Glover era, the epic and brilliant *Burn*.

The Montreux 1996 album features a set list that differs barely at all from the earliest Morse shows. Some of the more adventurous choices that grace *Live At The Olympia* — recorded earlier — are absent (the versions of 'Sometimes I Feel Like Screaming' and 'Fools' that end the CD are from the 2000 show). 'Fireball' is still present, as are 'Pictures Of Home' and 'When A Blindman Cries', but *Purpendicular* is ill-served ('The Purpendicular Waltz' survives and 'Cascades: I'm Not Your Lover' crops up on the expanded DVD version).

This can, in part, be put down to the time constraints attendant upon being part of a festival line-up, but it also anticipates a gradual erosion of the initial willingness to experiment that characterised Deep Purple's ascension back to being a full-on stadium act. Lord has spoken about audience expectations of what should be in a live show and how, if the band played everything that everyone wanted to hear, they would be on stage for four or five hours.[7]

Gillan explained in a 2013 interview how a setlist is arrived at: 'There are four elements to a Deep Purple show — old stuff, new stuff, obscure stuff and improvisation. A friend of mine came to two shows, Frankfurt and Hamburg and he said, you did the same set tonight as last night. I said, yeah, but last night was one hour forty-five minutes, tonight was two hours fifteen minutes. The same set, so that element of improvisation is what keeps it exciting.'[8]

As time went on, more recent material was increasingly de-emphasized and obscure songs made the cut less and less often. It is certainly the case that newer numbers have always been received by audiences with, at best, polite acceptance, bordering on indifference. The most egregious example of fan conservatism would come in 1999 at the Royal Albert Hall.

The Montreux show was part of what could very plausibly be called a world tour. This is a phrase that needs some unpacking. At the start of the band's career, in the late sixties and early seventies, a 'world tour' was nothing of the sort. With large chunks of the world off-limits for political reasons and others simply not geared up to host rock bands (even if their populations had had the first clue who those bands were), the 'world' for the purposes of live performance basically meant Western Europe, North America (not South America) and Japan. It is no accident that Deep Purple's most famous live album, the seminal *Made In Japan*, was recorded where it was. Even Anglophone countries such as Australia and New Zealand posed logistical difficulties that made rare stops of them.

By the mid-nineties, much had changed. Of particular significance for the band — as will become clear — was the collapse of the Soviet Union, which ushered in a slightly chaotic period during which formerly communist peoples acquired (although did not necessarily hang onto) many freedoms that they had hitherto lacked. Light was shone on places that had been dark and inaccessible for decades and that light revealed, as it happens, rather a lot of heavy rock, specifically Deep Purple, fans. A shift towards touring in Eastern Europe is a marked feature of the schedules from around this time. For example, the band played the Moscow Dynamo Stadium in June. They went on to appear in Tallinn, Estonia, on 5th July, Izola, Slovenia on 4th September and at the Central Republic

Stadium in Kyiv, Ukraine, on 13th September.[9]

Although the band saw out 1996 with dates in the old dependables, Japan and the USA, the new year would see them moving even further afield, not always with fortunate consequences. Breaking for Christmas, the band members — and their management — must have looked back on a generally successful year. The album had not done all that well, for sure, but it had driven a busy touring schedule that had resulted in the band reaching large numbers of fans all around the world. More importantly, it was very clear that a post-Blackmore age was not only possible, but an exciting and vibrant time to be alive.

The main question was, 'how long can it go on for?' This is a big one that has never satisfactorily been answered: every new Deep Purple album has had around it the aura of maybe/could be the final recorded output. Every tour has been supported by loyal fans wondering if this is their last chance to see their idols live. A Sword of Damocles engraved with the legend 'too old to rock and roll' has hung over everything the band has done. Yet, they didn't stop, they haven't stopped: they carried on for far longer than seemed likely during those early days of Steve Morse and *Purpendicular*.

3
A Band On

Deep Purple were very much a going concern, but they were also a long-standing institution and, as a new millennium approached, their past began to assume greater and greater importance. Anniversaries came and went, while demand for product — fuelled by the growing ease with which it could be accessed — increased. Over the coming years, new versions of older albums, rereleases of rare material and a bewildering array of live offerings would all hit the market, in an ultimately losing battle to satisfy the monstrous appetite of the fans. A key moment was reached in 1997 with the twenty fifth anniversary of their biggest seller, *Machine Head*.

'Anniversary Editions' of the old classics were not particularly a novelty. The earlier *In Rock* and *Fireball* albums had already received the deluxe treatment, both including not only remastered versions of the original songs, but remixes and — precious booty! — rare, or even previously lost, songs. *Machine Head* provided little of the latter, since the recording sessions had not produced much in the way of discarded ideas. 'When A Blindman Cries' gained its overdue promotion, but the archives threw up nothing else, other than alternative solos for some of the main songs, including 'Smoke On The Water'.

Anxious to give the fans something, Glover, who produced a disc of remixes to go alongside the main album, decided to be creative and included new finds from the original tapes with different solos. Not everyone was happy. Blackmore consulted lawyers over what he saw as unauthorised tampering with his work; his objections mysteriously went away when the anniversary edition proved to be quite a money spinner.

The 1997 touring season began with a date at the Estadio Santa Laura in Santiago de Chile on 27th February. It was to be a memorable night for a whole host of the wrong reasons.

Video clips of the event[1] show a huge crowd — Chile was one of the more modern additions to the tour schedule, but it was still a country teeming with Deep Purple fans. Clearly, any doubts the band and their management may have been having about their continued appeal were not borne out by the South American market.

As the band comes to the end of a version of what sounds like 'Into The Fire' from *In Rock*, a large number of fans climb a lighting tower that has been set up in the middle of the space, their aim presumably being to get a better view of the stage. As nothing more than a light scaffold intended to support a few lanterns and a couple of tech guys, the tower is simply not strong enough to take the weight of dozens of human bodies and, in one of those 'did I actually see what I thought I saw' moments, it collapses — straight on to the heads of the surrounding crowd.

Miraculously, no one was killed, but forty-four people were injured.[2] Understandably, the shocked band left the stage, in the belief, no doubt, that the concert was, as of that moment, cancelled. That was not the opinion of the organisers, who, fearing the retribution of an angry mob — or financial ruin — insisted on a resumption. Allegedly, the band were already in their van ready for the drive back to their hotel when they were hastily bundled back onstage.[3] The interruption had lasted for forty minutes — a modest amount of time, given what had happened.

Amazingly, that was not the night's only controversy. Outside the stadium, local police were forced to use water cannons to keep at bay swarms of people who, having missed out on tickets, were attempting to storm the turnstiles. Meanwhile, inside, Steve Morse was nearly getting into a physical altercation with an alleged fan. The person in question was situated close to the stage and had spent much of the (truncated) gig flipping the finger at Steve and even spitting on him.

It can only be posited that he was one of the Blackmore die-hards who would bedevil Morse throughout his tenure with the band. The final note played, the guitarist jumped down into the audience and proceeded to take issue with his tormenter. Only the quick thinking of some on-hand stewards prevented a fight from breaking out.[4] It can only be posited that the usually laid-back Morse had been made uncharacteristically excitable by the febrile atmosphere.

In fairness, there are those who maintain that spitting is a mark of respect in Chile. The then Rainbow singer Doogie White is said to have suffered similar treatment to that of Morse, although, since he may have been singing one of *Stranger In Us All*'s less memorable songs at the time, it proves very little either way. None of this, of course, exculpates a fan who was also giving Morse the middle finger salute throughout the show.

The tour continued with stops in Argentina, Brazil, Peru, Bolivia and Venezuela. Some of these involved multiple nights at a single venue, further hinting at the band's popularity. The South American leg of the tour concluded at the end of March; the next dates were in Europe in July. The reason for this was simple: a new album was being prepared.

In some respects, this is surprising. It does not match the band's output in the late sixties and early seventies, when they managed, in one surge of activity, to complete three albums in twelve months, but it is certainly more productive than had been the case of late. Since reforming in 1984, Deep Purple had been releasing new material at the rate of an album every three years or so. To be back in the studio while *Purpendicular* was still young enough to qualify as the 'new' album suggested a renewed level of creativity not seen for quite a while.

The first sessions were held in June, Glover giving an upbeat report: 'No title has yet been decided, although there are several on the table, one or two under the table, a few beneath the cushion of a cheap chair, one caught on the horn of a suspicious looking ram on a remote ranch in New Zealand (no idea how it got there!), four were inadvertently washed in some jeans, and US Customs seized seven. That leaves several.'[5]

He added, 'Jon is finishing work already in progress and so therefore we are all meeting up again alarmingly soonish after the Summer gig things to complete the writing and recording, not to mention the strudel.'[6] The tone is comical — sometimes, by Glover's own admission, sarcastic — but it masks an emerging trend that was to have bigger consequences down the line. The mention of Lord working on a different project is a throwaway, but it was much more serious than Glover realised.

The project occupying Lord was a solo album, *Pictured Within*, which had had a lengthy gestation period: as Lord said: 'For the last fifteen years, I guess, I've been jotting down ideas, fragments, possibilities and a couple of years ago, it actually started to fall into shape and make sense.'[7] That he was engaged in such activity was newsworthy in itself.

As a writer, he had been less than prolific since his early seventies classical experiments. His one solo product, *Before I Forget*, from 1982, had belied its title by having slipped from the collective memory. His post-1984 credits on Deep Purple albums had been few and far between (apart from on the 'all for one and one for all' statement that was *Purpendicular*). Blackmore actually bemoaned Lord's lack of input: 'I don't know why, to this day, he doesn't come up with any ideas. I still find that awesome — that he still doesn't come up with one idea. It's very odd.'[8]

Released a year after its recording, *Pictured Within* is a collection of largely instrumental pieces that, Lord claimed, were broadly autobiographical, although more in an affective than narrative manner. Elgar's 'Enigma Variations' are the inspiration for both the title and the form of what was conceived as a series of connected pieces. The three vocal tracks are 'Evening Song' and 'Wait a While', sung by Lord's family friend Sam Brown, and the title track, which is essayed by Miller Anderson, a blues guitarist and singer who had been plying his trade since way back when. The album as a whole is not classical in style, although it does feature some classical musicians to go along with the core sounds of electronic keyboards, percussion and electronic bass. The main instrument, though, is the piano, played by Lord.

The album wears the commitment that went into making it on its sleeve. The tunes have clearly not emerged from jams, as has always been the case with Deep Purple. They have been carefully composed and, as per their remit, are evocative of moods and sensations. A good deal of meditative melancholy comes through, often carried by a folky fiddle. Nothing sounds like rock 'n' roll. More often, it could be mistaken for incidental music from a film or television programme; sometimes, it is almost ambient. It is beautiful, elegant and an eloquent response to Blackmore's criticisms. It is not easy to see it appealing to the average Deep Purple fan — which may have been part of the point. Its recording was one of two things that happened in 1997 that caused Lord to begin to conceive of a future very different from that for which he seemed destined — of rock keyboard player winding down to retirement.

But the future was for the future: there was much to do in the present. Not least, there was more touring, this time in Europe. Then, in September, everyone assembled at Greg Rike Studios for more new album sessions. If Glover's first studio report had been bullish about how quickly progress could be made, it was not matched by experience. Recording would drag on until February of the following year. September also saw the appearance of another solo outing by a member of the band, one which, in its own way, would have as much longer-term influence as *Pictured Within*.

As Lord was finalising a project that had gone back years, the workaholic Gillan had also been indulging his muse, but had chosen his usual 'there and then' approach to getting tings done. The result was a work as steeped in wider influences and creative energy as anything his Deep Purple colleague was doing.

Unfortunately, *Dreamcatcher* has come to be considered Gillan's most obscure album, an oddity that failed to excite critics and sold in such low volumes that it is now almost impossible to obtain. Long since deleted, even picking up a second-hand copy is difficult — for something to be second-hand, it needs to have been bought in the first place.

Gillan's only collaborator on it was Steve Morris — not to be confused with the guitarist in his day job band. An old pal of the singer, Morris had first entered Gillan's life in 1989, when he had played guitar on a tour with a Gillan non-Purple group called Garth Rockett and the Moonshiners. From there, he had been chief player and main songwriting partner on *Naked Thunder* and *Toolbox*.

Gillan has stated that, apart from Glover, Morris is his longest-standing writing partner.[9] Morris described the process in relation to *Dreamcatcher*: 'Writing with Ian is great. I can come up with the strangest idea and he'll find something in it and create a song. A case in point is 'Chandra's Coriander'. I had done a session in London, and the engineer who had recently recorded the Pogues, gave me a stereo mix of the Irish Percussion. It sounded great on its own, but I put an acoustic track over it. It felt really good, so I played it to Ian, and he started working on it. We finished the song in Portugal, where in an Indian Restaurant run by Chandra, Ian introduced me to the Coriander, and before you know it, it's the title!'[10]

Of the album's overall failure, he opined, 'I really like *Dreamcatcher*, but it's not to everybody's taste. They seem to want Ian to sing 'Rock' on every album, but that is so limiting. Lots of different styles out there guys, and Ian wants to experiment on his solo records.'[11]

The album is definitely experimental. There is some rock-inflected material, such as 'Hard on You', but, mostly, it references blues, folk, even world music. 'Chandra's Coriander' is a lively start, 'That's Why God is Singing the Blues' is an environmental protest song with some of Gillan's wittier lyrics, while 'You Sold My Love For A Song' is wistful blues. Two songs would go on to have long afterlives: 'Sugar Plum' — in severely rocked-up form — would become a mainstay of Gillan's solo live shows, as would 'A Day Late And A Dollar Short', which he would describe as a favourite among the countless songs that he has written, or co-written.[12]

As much as it qualifies as one of Gillan's minor works, *Dreamcatcher* — as Morris astutely realised — speaks to a growing desire on the singer's part to push beyond the boundaries of the career that he had built for himself. When Lord had presented Deep Purple with his *Concerto for Group and Orchestra* in 1969, Gillan had been one of the most vocal naysayers, arguing that the band was heavy rock and nothing more. This view did not last for long. He did the *Jesus Christ Superstar* thing before fronting a Purple hiatus band, named after himself, that produced three albums of jazz-fusion rock. Moving into the later stages of his career, his interest in working with musicians of a different hue, and in other genres, was only increasing.

Work on Deep Purple's new album was interrupted by a tour of House of Blues venues in the US. A venture invested in by such unlikely business partners as Dan Aykroyd and Harvard University, House of Blues is a chain of restaurants-cum-concert halls that take many of their design cues from Aykroyd's fading film classic *The Blues Brothers*. At several sites, the band played short residencies lasting several nights. The decision to take on this tour no doubt came, again, from a lack of certainty about the band's capacity to pull in large crowds in North America. It also had the infelicitous effect of reducing them to being a glorified cabaret act, providing a musical backdrop to burgers and fries.

The set lists allowed for some tentative experimentation, but erred towards the safe. The opener was 'Hush', a huge hit in the US for the Mark I iteration of the band (which did not include Gillan and Glover) in 1968. Bringing it back was Morse's idea — an inspired one as it has remained on the set list ever since. Other songs mostly came from the early seventies' albums. *Purpendicular* was barely represented at all — the beginning of its slide into live performance extinction — while audiences were treated to something from the forthcoming album in the form of 'Seventh Heaven'. The tour went on into the early months of 1998, interspersed with more work on the new album.

From a long-term perspective, the most notable feature of the House of Blues tour was that it included two 'cybercasts' of concerts from Los Angeles and Las Vegas. The Internet had not been a thing when the band reformed in 1984 and was not especially influential in 1993. In 1998, it still had a 'shock of the new' glamour, but it would become more important to the band — as to everyone else — as time went on.

The new album was released in May 1998 under the title *Abandon*, sometimes rendered as A.Band.On. It was the second album running with a single word punning title, this one more successful than that given to its predecessor. On the one hand, it refers to a feeling of unbridled joy, on the other, it is the statement 'a band on' as in, 'a band working at the top of their game'. In a third sense, it would be applied to live dates, which were trailed as 'a band on tour'.

The label was EMI, BMG (who had underwritten the

previous couple of albums) having lost interest in the light of disappointing chart positions. The new home — a coming home, as all of Deep Purple's sixties and seventies albums were from the EMI stable — was evident in the greater premium placed on the visuals. Gone was the 'back of a fag packet' approach that had been taken with *Purpendicular* to be replaced by — discuss! — the band's most slickly designed packaging ever (although *The House of Blue Light* runs it a close second).

The front cover shows a man in *Speedos* diving to nowhere against the backdrop of a modern American cityscape, all given a frosty blue wash. It certainly looks expensive, although not as iconic as may have been intended.

Another difference from *Purpendicular* is the music's relative lack of diversity. An acoustic-inflected diversion into folk with 'Fingers To The Bone' aside, this album is heavy and intense, although Gillan denied that it was heavy metal: 'I used to get so angry when we were described as a heavy metal band, for the simple reason that 'heavy metal' is the least musical phrase I've ever heard in my life and, without being too pompous about it, Purple has got some musical ability: the guys can play.'[13]

Proceedings get off to an uncompromising start with a drum beat and a moody, growling Hammond organ, as 'Any Fule Kno That' (the title taken from the classic satire on public school life, 'Molesworth') throws the unsuspecting listener in head first. From there, it never really lets up. Yes, there are a couple of ballads, 'Don't Make Me Happy' and, to some extent, 'Seventh Heaven', but they are heavy ballads. Even 'Fingers To The Bone' is based not around its twiddly Celtic main riff, but pounding fuzzbox-heavy chords backed up by an immense quantity of bass.

It is all very entertaining — indeed, it has improved over time as the subtleties that were not obvious on an initial spin have revealed themselves with repeated listening — but it cannot be described as progress. As if to underline the point, the album ends with a remake of 'Blooduscker', a track from *In Rock*, now inexplicably retitled, 'Bludsucker'.

Two areas are worthy of comment, the lyrics and Jon Lord's role. Of the former, it can only be said that the album is something of a low. There is a worrying preponderance of clichés among the song titles. While the problem is nowhere near as acute as it was on *The Battle Rages On…*, the likes of 'Watching The Sky', 'Fingers To The Bone', 'Seventh Heaven' and even 'Whatsername' do not bode well. More serious are the lyrics, which veer between the meaningless and the banal.

Gillan has often stated that the important thing with lyrics is that they sound good, that they must have a 'percussive texture and be delivered in the rhythm section as part of the band. So you can sing almost anything so long as it sounds good in a rock song, but, you've got to have a good title — and then the fun starts, because then you've got to have a focus, because it has got to sound good. You've got to mean it — and if you mean it, you've got to think, "well I've got to have a focus on this somehow." So, when we're writing, we always have, "what is this song about?" and even if it's a nebulous sort of lyric, even if it's a sort of abstract or avant-garde approach to things, saying nothing, even if the only value of a lyric is as a word exercise, rhymes and things, we have to have a meaning.'[14]

In a sense, he is saying that lyrics should have the value of musical notes, adding to the aural qualities of a song. That can be seen in 'Any Fule Kno That':

'Oh Moronica Queen of the Biz
And her friend Flash Harry
thinks he knows what it is
Tin Pan Alley Fat Head Larry don't know shit'

Here, the concatenating assonance, the wordplay and the sprung rhythms certainly make for an arresting pattern of words

— a clever pattern, too — that add to the overall soundscape, but Gillan's claims about meaning notwithstanding, there is no story, no theme. Deep Purple nonsense songs are a tradition — with Mark II anyway — but there is a point at which the joke starts to wear thin and several entries on the *Abandon* track list are wilfully devoid of all sense.

At the other end of the spectrum are songs that mean something, but it is rarely a very interesting something. The autobiographical '69' works well enough, but the 'voice of the working man' pose that Gillan adopts in 'Fingers To The Bone' would sound more convincing coming from Kenny Rogers or Johnny Cash.

A good question might be, 'so what?' If lyrical coherence were a criterion for a song's success, most of popular music would fail. No song has ever been criticised primarily for its lyrics. Still, whoever came up with that verse from 'Any Fule' is clearly a skilful writer and more ought to be expected from them.

Musically, the album is excellent. On the whole it sticks to familiar paths, with many songs resembling those on *Purpendicular*, or earlier albums, in structure, if not in style. A notable feature is how the arrangements very often foreground Lord's keyboards. He is the first lead musician to be heard and the opening song features a no-nonsense Hammond organ solo: it is only one of several granted to the maestro, a lovely wistful electric piano turn in 'Fingers To The Bone' being an album highlight.

It is ironic, then, that just as Lord was re-establishing himself within the band, a young man in the Netherlands named Marco de Goeij asked to meet him and, from that moment on, his departure was only a matter of time.

Former Dixie Dregs and Kansas guitarist, Steve Morse take his place in the Deep Purple ranks during the very first press conference with the new line-up at the Presidente Hotel in Mexico City, 23rd November 1994. No one at the time could have foreseen that Morse would remain Deep Purple's guitarist for nearly thirty years.
(RTAceves / MediaPunch Inc / Alamy Stock Photo)

Following the departure of Blackmore in 1993, it wasn't until early 1996 that Purple returned to playing the UK, promoting the critically acclaimed Purpendicular. Coincidentally the London shows were at the same venue, the Brixton Academy in March.
(Mel Longhurst / Alamy Stock Photo)

An intense moment with Steve, Wembley Arena, London, 14th October 1998. The day had started with the band appearing on Channel 4 TV's *The Big Breakfast* performing 'Black Night' and 'Smoke On The Water.'
(Mel Longhurst / Alamy Stock Photo)

Following the success of the 30th anniversary "Concerto" performances at the Royal Albert Hall, the following year, the highly ambitious decision was made to take an orchestra on the road. These photos are from the Fila Forum, Assago, Milan on 23rd October 2000. Aside from the Romanian Philarmonic Orchestra, old friend Ronnie James Dio was amongst the supporting cast.

(Fabio Diena / Alamy Stock Photo)

Touring the States. HiFi Buys Amphitheatre, Atlanta, Georgia, 19th June 2002.
(Chris McKay / MediaPunch Inc / Alamy Stock Photo)

Gillan and Morse at Hammersmith, 6th September 2002. The band had played the same venue in February for Lord's final gigs, but with Gillan suffering with a bad cold, and others in the band also ill, the rest of the tour was put back to later in the year. By the time of the rescheduled shows Don Airey was established as the keyboard player but these UK gigs featured a guest appearance by Jon Lord, who took over for the second half of the shows, with the final one in Ipswich on 19th September.
(Simon Meaker / Alamy Stock Photo)

Steve Morse at the Pavarotti and Friends charity concert in Modena, Italy, 27th May 2003.
(dpa picture alliance / Alamy Stock Photo)

Morse and Glover during the presentation of *Bananas* in Berlin, 20th August 2003.
(dpa picture alliance / Alamy Stock Photo)

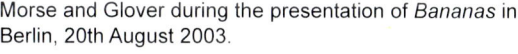

Above: Stadio Sinigaglia, Como, 13th July 2004.
(Fabio Diena / Alamy Stock Photo)

Ian Gillan at Live 8 Canada in Barrie, Ontario on 2nd July 2005.
(UPI Photo / Grace Chiu / Alamy Stock Photo)

Jon Lord reunited with Ian Paice and Ian Gillan for the Classic Rock Roll of Honour Awards, at the Cafe de Paris, London, 4th October 2005.
(Yui Mok / Press Association / Alamy Stock Photo)

Teatro Ventaglio Smeraldo, Milan, 15th July 2008.
(Massimo Barbaglia / MARKA / Alamy Stock Photo)

(From left to right): Radio presenter Bob Harris and TV presenter Esther Rantzen with Jon Lord at the first Childline Rocks concert at the IndigO2 in London, 1st June 2009. This event saw Lord reunite with Glenn Hughes, performing 'You Keep On Moving' and 'Mistreated' with the "house" band Thunder.

(Zak Hussein / Press Association / Alamy Stock Photo)

4
A Load Of Orchestras

Over a long career, Jon Lord had many 'finest moments' — the riff to 'Child In Time', perhaps, or the stunning opening to the song 'Perfect Strangers' — but none was finer than the *Concerto for Group and Orchestra*. A fifty minute-plus melding of rock and classical music, it is a masterpiece of creativity, elan, ambition and sheer bloody mindedness. Its first — and for many years only, in its complete form — performance took place in September 1969 at the Royal Albert Hall in London, and featured Deep Purple in collaboration with the Royal Philharmonic Orchestra. It is one of the stranger Deep Purple pub quiz answers that a recording of the event became the first full length release for the Mark II version of the band.

It had not been popular with most of Lord's colleagues. Blackmore, in particular, had been very opposed (although, ever the professional, his parts were immaculately played). As has been said already, Gillan, too, was not that keen. Their contention — a not entirely unreasonable one — was that Deep Purple was a rock band, so what were they doing messing around with orchestras? Although they were cajoled into a couple more such exercises, classical crossovers were quickly removed from the band's repertoire.

It many ways, this didn't matter, because the score for the 'Concerto' was, in any case, lost. Without it, a repetition was impossible. It is hard to fathom how something so catastrophic could have happened. Presumably, there were many copies of the score — or, at least, different instrumental parts — in 1969, but they all mysteriously disappeared. Paul Mann — who would become a significant figure in the history of the 'Concerto' — agreed: 'It remains even to this day a mystery. Nothing has been found. The best that we could come up with was that probably when the [partial revival] LA performances finished [in 1970}, it probably came back to London and was put in to the office in London, which became the Purple office and when the Purple office closed, probably it was thrown out.'[1]

According to Mann, Lord himself attempted to reconstruct the score over the years, but with little success: 'Jon tried a couple of times to do it himself. He was getting so many requests from people to play the 'Concerto' but in the end I think he just gave up because it was too time-consuming to contemplate that amount of work, especially as he was all the time on the road with Deep Purple.'[2]

This is the point at which Marco de Goeij entered the picture. Born in 1967 in Gouda in the Netherlands, he was a serious student of music and a composer in his own right. He has spoken of how he developed an early love for classical music, but was also taken with rock, the defining moment coming when his brother turned up with some Deep Purple albums and stuck them on the turntable. They included the 'Concerto', with which Marco became immediately fascinated.[3]

He was particularly intrigued by the Tchaikovsky influences that he detected in the classical sections. He takes up the story, 'I was at college and I wanted to write some sort of paper or thesis about [the Concerto] and I found out that there wasn't a score available and that was the moment when I toyed with the idea of transcribing it. I knew it was going to be a lot of work.'[4]

That was putting it mildly. Furthermore, there was a time pressure: the thirtieth anniversary of the first performance was coming up and what better way to celebrate than to recreate it? The initiative for this came from an unexpected source, as Lord explained: 'The rest of the band, actually — it wasn't I who said, "let's do its thirtieth birthday." It was the rest of the band who said, "wouldn't it be a good idea" — well, after I had wired my jaw back up, "huh? You want to do the 'Concerto'?", because they'd famously dissed it in the past.'[5] But a new performance could not be contemplated without the score. It all came down to the score.

De Goeij's main worry at the start of the process was the possibility that he could complete eighty to ninety percent of the work, only for someone to turn up with a rediscovered copy of the original, rendering all of his efforts vain. Thus, his first job was to definitively establish that it really was irretrievably lost. 'I wrote a letter to Sir Malcolm Arnold' he said, 'I thought that was a good point to start, because he conducted it [in 1969]. It was obvious that Jon [Lord] didn't have a copy, so I thought Sir Malcolm Arnold was a good point to start and I got a reaction — he said that the location of the scores was not his responsibility and he didn't have a copy.'[6] Other investigations proved equally fruitless, so the Herculean labour of transcribing began.

It was painstaking work. Do Goeij's only sources were the recording of the original performance together with a film version of it. His method was to listen and try to write down what he heard, while, where possible, watching what the musicians were doing in order to get a sense of any notes that he missed, as well as to gain an understanding of the orchestration. This was, it can be guessed, more of a challenge for the classical parts than those supplied by the band, many of which were — mercifully, he must have thought — improvised. He decided to approach Lord when he had completed around 60% of the work, with a full score of the second movement (of three) done, along with a lot of the third movement and a piano-only sketch of the first movement.

Knowing that Deep Purple were due to play the Rotterdam Ahoy on 12th October 1998[7], he made a trip to that city, taking his work-in-progress. Identifying the hotel in which he thought it most likely that Lord was staying, he left a note at the reception, explaining who he was and what he had done, appending an extract from the score as proof. It was not needed. As he left the hotel, a car pulled up outside, which disgorged on to the street Gillan and the man himself, Jon Lord. Conscious of the risk of coming across as a star-struck fan hanging around for an autograph, De Goeij realised that his window for getting Lord's attention was small, especially as the keyboardist was not in the best of moods.

Lord's recollection (he placed the incident in February of 1999) was of having been driven at scary speeds from somewhere in Germany, 'I was ragged, you know, and I got out and this young man came up to me and said, "Mr Lord, may I talk to you a minute?" And I was like — I want a cup of tea, man! And I want a shower and I'm sorry, but we've got a concert in an hour and I was just — no way. I was doing a David Coverdale, you know, flipping my hair back and he said, "it's about your *Concerto for Group and Orchestra.*" So — sit down, young man. I said, "what about it?" And he said, "I think I've managed to recreate most of it."'[8]

The two drank some coffee together and started to go through what De Goeij had brought with him. He had produced a computer-based score, but it brought back to Lord memories of his handwritten original: he even claimed that he could see again the coffee stains from the many cups that had sustained him through nights of writing after days spent rehearsing, writing and perfecting the magnum opus that is *Deep Purple In Rock*.

Suddenly, the mooted thirtieth anniversary revival was a very real possibility, but, more than that, as De Goeij explained, 'It made [Lord] realise that he had to follow his own path, or own career, playing the things that he liked and doing the things that he liked, like playing with orchestras.'[9]

That conversation, so easily overlooked or dismissed, was a watershed in the history of Deep Purple. Lord was a founding member of the band — he and Ian Paice were the only founding members left. He had appeared on every Deep Purple album, played at every gig. When Blackmore left in 1993, he, too, had been around since the start, but he had not been a constant presence — *Come Taste The Band* is eloquent testimony to that. Lord was the bedrock, the calming, diplomatic presence who had kept everything moving forward, as rickety and gaffer-taped together as it was. Yet, here he was, on the cusp of a decision that would change the band forever.

Still, before that could happen, the new 'Concerto' needed to become a reality, so De Goeij went off to complete his work and Lord continued on tour with Deep Purple. In May 1999, two years of something close to obsession came to an end: De Goeij called on Lord at home, full score in his bag, ready to present it to its creator. The two went through it, making corrections where they seemed merited. Lord wanted to update the piece, which took up June and July. He and De Goeij met up again in August, in, of all places, Birmingham Airport, to go through Lord's corrections. With these fed into De Goeij's computer, the score was ready for performance — almost.

Enter the third important figure in this story, the aforementioned Paul Mann. Educated at Chetham School of Music and York University, he was hailed, even back in 1999, as a talent to watch, having won the prestigious Donatello Flick Conducting Competition a year earlier. Of course, a true thirtieth anniversary of the 'Concerto' would have seen the return of the original conductor, Sir Malcolm Arnold, but he had been in poor health for years and was being cared for by a loyal companion in Norfolk. His participation was thus not only unlikely, but virtually impossible (he died in 2006). Mann, then, was a fine choice to step into his — very big — shoes.

Lord told a story of how Mann's desire to be a conductor

originated when his childhood self 'air conducted' his mother's recording of *Concerto for Group and Orchestra* using one of her knitting needles (painted white) as a baton.[10]

Mann had actually been involved with Lord for some time: 'I was on at Jon for years to actually do it again, long before we ever actually did it. The first time I met Jon to talk about it would have been about '93, something like that. I met him backstage after a show. Initially, he was a bit, "why do you want to do that?" You know, "what for?" I think it took him a while to come round to the idea.'[11]

It should be noted that Mann was the nephew of Colin Hart, Deep Purple's tour manager, hence his ready access to the band. Given his achievements in classical music, this can be called serendipity, rather than nepotism. 'Apparently', Mann explained, 'on one of those long tour bus journeys, when they were discussing the idea of doing it again, back in — I suppose it would have been around '98 on the 'Abandon' tour, the subject came to, well yeah, if we're going to do it, who are we going to get to conduct it? I think Colin said something like, well, my nephew's a conductor. I think it was Ian Gillan who said, "yeah, I think we're going to need someone a bit better than just a member of your family, Colin."'[12]

Mann not only brought himself to the project, but also the orchestra with which he had been extensively working — the London Symphony — and a host of suggestions and ideas. He helped to give the piece its final polish, as he said: 'Between the 1969 and the 1999 one, there were a lot of changes. Jon made a couple of cuts, tightened the structure in a few places, and made a few quite substantial alterations to some sections, including adding an extra verse in the second movement. In the 1999 version he also goes twice round the Hammond tune near the beginning of the third movement, where in the 1969 it's only once. There are various things like that.'[13]

The rehearsals this time were much more enjoyable than

had been the case in 1969. This was largely because attitudes had changed and the old antagonism between classical and popular musicians was no longer so much in evidence. Lord remarked upon this, 'In that intervening thirty years, some sort of sea change had happened with orchestras... orchestras are much more open-minded. They see much more that brotherhood of musicians I see, that they didn't thirty years before.'[14]

Mann remembers the rehearsals vividly: 'The first rehearsal that we had — which was in a little studio in Putney — there's a photo of us somewhere and I was trying to play the orchestral part on a piano and the band were playing to learn the cues. That was my first experience of watching them work. The incredible kind of closeness and swiftness of communication that existed between them.'[15]

The partnership between Mann and Lord was particularly fruitful, Mann describing it as: 'Jon and I — without — again without really sitting down and talking about it, working it who would say what and do what, we just managed to combine, so Jon was speaking to the band in their language and I was speaking to the orchestra in their language, and somehow we were all understanding each other in a really mutually effective way.'[16]

Two concerts were scheduled (it was originally intended to be one, but public demand necessitated the adding of a second) for the 25th and 26th of September — thirty years almost to the day since the original performance. The venue was again, the Royal Albert Hall. The programme consisted not merely of a Deep Purple gig with the addition of the 'Concerto'; instead, the opportunity was taken to make the event a more wide-ranging celebration of the band and its 'family'. The first half consisted of various guest stars essaying songs and tunes from disparate side projects. Miller Anderson and Sam Brown popped up to give lovely renditions of their songs from *Pictured Within*, Steve Morris supported Gillan in a version of 'That's

Why God Is Singing The Blues', Ronnie James Dio, erstwhile singer with Rainbow (and Gillan's predecessor in Black Sabbath) helped Glover out with a couple of numbers from *The Butterfly Ball* and Steve Morse did a brace of Dixie Dregs instrumentals, including 'Take It Off The Top'.

The most curious, and in some ways revealing, contribution came from Ian Paice. With little in the way of a solo catalogue to draw upon, he elected to rejig the Mark I Deep Purple classic 'Wring That Neck' as a horns-led jazz piece: it worked surprisingly well, hinting, perhaps at the musical variety that had always lain under the surface of Deep Purple's output.

The 'Concerto' dominated the second half. Listening to the recording of this performance alongside that from 1969 is a fascinating experience. The orchestral parts are obviously fixed and, better recording technology aside, are much the same as they ever were. That cannot be said of the band's efforts. Morse's guitar is more distorted than was Blackmore's, which gives the sound a heavier — and more contemporary — feel. He also never imitates, or even tries to imitate, Blackmore: his solos sound like Morse and no-one else. The result is that the band's parts are more assuredly Mark II Deep Purple in quality than was the case first time around, the 'Concerto' having been written with the differently-styled Mark I in mind.

Only Glover's at times too 'groovy' bass line has anything distinctively sixties about it. Gillan's vocals in the second movement are not perhaps quite as 'pure' as they were, but that is more than made up for with the drama and commitment that he gets into his performance. What flirted with querulousness in 1969 is now heartfelt and moving.

An issue — certainly at the first of the two concerts — was so-called fans calling out for the band to play some of their heavy rock classics. This became very annoying very quickly, although one wag did request 'Stonehenge' — possibly the track from Gillan's Black Sabbath album, but more likely the deliberately pompous *Spinal Tap* shambles. 'What we later discovered had happened,' Mann has said, 'it was actually a good lesson for the future on the tour as well, is that I think some people had seen the posters outside the Albert Hall and went, oh look, Deep Purple, with a symphony orchestra. Then when they found out that they had to sit there quietly, listening to music you know, played by an orchestra, their expectations were obviously not fulfilled.'[17]

It became so distracting that a visibly shaken Lord took up the mic between movements to chastise the hecklers; the overwhelming support that he received from the majority of the audience must have made him feel a bit better. But the fact that such drastic action was necessary speaks to an inherent conservatism among some sections of the Deep Purple fan base that has not improved over time — if anything, it has got worse. The rowdy contingent sort-of got their wish later when the band played a brief orchestra-backed set, which consisted of a couple of older songs, but mainly showcased *Purpendicular* and *Abandon*.

Notwithstanding any of that, the concerts were a triumph. The 'come one, come all' singalong of 'Smoke On The Water' that brought proceedings to a close was the perfect encapsulation of the spirit: inclusive, celebratory. Lord later revealed that a constituency which especially enjoyed it was the orchestra, 'Even the older members of the orchestra were coming up, shaking our hands, getting autographs and so on… probably because they're the same generation as me.'[18]

Mann also spoke of how members of the orchestra remembered the concert as a highlight of their careers — to the extent of still mentioning it years after the event.

A recording of the second show was prepared for release almost immediately. As early as 26th October, Glover was giving an update on progress: 'I've just returned from a week spent in Peter Gabriel's Real World Studios in Wiltshire, mixing the RAH recording. Jon and IG were there also, IP popped in and Paul Mann came for a couple of days, helping with the 'Concerto' mix. It was a great week, good teamwork, and it's all coming together very well.'[19]

Despite having once again put on the mantel of being Deep Purple's sugar daddies, EMI turned down the opportunity to release the 'Concerto' album following poor sales for *Abandon*. It was the beginning of a rift between band and label that was to end unhappily some years down the line. The recently-formed Eagle Rock stepped in and agreed to take the 'Concerto' recording on, allegedly paying the kind of huge advance that those more experienced in the industry might have more cannily haggled over.

As it happened, at around the same time, they signed that other old rock edifice Status Quo, also apparently for a huge advance. The resulting album, *Under The Influence*, sank like a Rolls Royce in a swimming pool. The company faced an early existential crisis, but were saved by surprisingly strong sales for the DVD and CD of the 'Concerto'. In fact, the 'Concerto' releases did so well that they were a major contributor to Eagle's establishing themselves as big players on the recording scene.

A wonderful diversion, the 'Concerto' was left behind as the new year – and new millennium - rolled around, bringing with it business as usual. More touring was planned — sending the band to Australia and Japan. Various releases were in the pipeline, including an anniversary edition of Mark II's album, *Who Do We Think We Are*, a recording of an Australian gig from 1999 under the title of *Total Abandon* (which has come to be regarded as a modern classic live album), as well as the recording of the 'Concerto' revival. Gillan was promising a new studio album, but none was to be forthcoming that year, or, indeed, any year for quite a while to come.

That is not to say that no new material was written. In July, the band returned — again — to the Montreux Jazz Festival for what proved to be one of their more intriguing gigs. During the afternoon sound check, Morse started to play a riff, others joined in, Gillan improvised some lyrics and — hey presto! — a song was born.[20]

'Long Time Gone' was played that night (and probably in Spain a couple of nights later) and has been ignored by the band ever since. It has never been officially recorded, although the question as to whether it might be has often been asked — a flat 'no' being the habitual response. This is a pity, because it is a thoroughly enjoyable piece of catchy blues rock, enlivened by some excellent solos. Now a semi-mythical part of the Deep Purple story, if it did nothing else, it suggested that creativity was not in short supply, making the long delay before the next studio album doubly difficult to understand.

Still, the 'Concerto' was not quite done with and September saw the start of a group and orchestra tour — or rather, two tours, one in South America and one in Europe. Mann described how these came about: 'It was actually at the Albert Hall, after the second show, we were sitting in the bar backstage at the Albert Hall and somebody said, wouldn't it be… we should tour this. We should take this out. And, of course, [the band's manager] Bruce Payne was there and I remember him looking, really, are you serious? You know how complicated this is, how expensive this is — it's just ridiculous! No chance.'[21] Treated as no more than a pipe dream, a flood of offers from all over the world to do such a tour prompted a rethink.

It was less a series of Deep Purple gigs than the Albert Hall experience on the road. Some elements were dropped — Sam Brown was presumably not available, but Dio was there, his slot expanding to include both the *Butterfly Ball* songs and two of his solo pieces, 'Fever Dreams' and 'Rainbow In The Dark'.

Miller Anderson did 'Pictured Within' (surely the least work that anyone has ever had to do in return for a trip around the world). Gillan gave audiences 'That's Why God…', without

Steve Morris, and 'Via Miami', which had originally appeared on his and Glover's *Accidentally On Purpose* album.

The jazzy 'Wring That Neck' made a welcome return. The main event was, naturally enough, the 'Concerto', followed again by a handful of Deep Purple songs — with an emphasis on newer material.

Although the Romanian Philharmonic were the partners of choice for most of the dates, local orchestras were booked in at some locations. An example was the Buenos Aires Symphony Orchestra, the first stop being in another country rarely, if ever, visited in the old days, Argentina.

As in London, the show was performed for two consecutive nights at the Luna Park. The Deep Purple Appreciation Society's magazine *Darker Than Blue* said of these, '[group and orchestra stepped out] in front of something like 8,000 people. Of this huge audience, only a few seemed intent on spoiling it, shouting during 'Pictured Within' and the 'Concerto'. During the Third Movement, they became so bad that Mann was forced to ask for silence.'[22]

Sadly, similar audience behaviour marred the three shows in Sao Paolo that came next. Appeasing this small, but vocal, minority no doubt lay behind the decision to feature more rock material as the tour moved over to Europe. The problem was not merely the classical music, but the fact that Dio was there, a singer whose trade was heavy metal in the way that Deep Purple's was not and who had his own following.

'One of the many things Ian Gillan should be credited with,' Mann has said, 'is the shape and the form that the concerts took. He realised quite early on that the idea that we had originally — the idea was to start with a little piece of classical music, a little short brilliant, classical showpiece, then to play the 'Concerto'… and then put all the rock stuff, all the crossover stuff in the second half and it was Ian who took the lead in saying it's a mistake to dive straight into the 'Concerto' to make the audience sit concentratedly for so long.'[23]

The European leg began in Antwerp, Belgium, on 30th September. Extra nights were added in some locations. A date at the Rotterdam Ahoy in October was recorded and given an official release; its enhanced rock section included the likes of 'Fools', 'Perfect Strangers', 'Black Night', 'Highway Star' and 'When A Blindman Cries' — the last of these definitely benefiting from orchestral accompaniment. Mystifyingly, the performance of the 'Concerto' from that night was not included on the album, for, apparently, 'legal reasons', although a power failure may have been the true culprit.[24]

Planned dates in the USA did not happen, but, in the early months of 2001, the orchestra was back for a couple of nights in Japan that were appended to the band's Australia tour. One of these, recorded in Tokyo on 25th March, appeared as part of a series of releases that went under the blanket title of the *Soundboard Series*. This also included recordings from other locations, such as Hong Kong. Most have been put out again some twenty years on as stand-alone packages.

The Tokyo performance features a similar set to that played at the Rotterdam Ahoy — with the addition of the 'Concerto'. Notable is the song 'Perfect Strangers'. Already a heavy masterpiece, the addition of the orchestra transforms it into a musical epic. The lyrics — standard Gillan nonsense in their basic form — become genuinely poetic when set against the backing of strings and brass provided by — in this instance — the Shin Nihon Philharmonic Select Orchestra.

The orchestra tour served a number of purposes. On the one hand, it allowed those fans — the clear majority — who were unable to attend the Royal Albert Hall 'Concerto' revival to get a flavour of the occasion. On another, it demonstrated again that Deep Purple, at their heart, have never been the complacent nostalgia band for which they are often taken. Experimentation drives everything they do — in the post-Blackmore age, at least.

The orchestra tour was by no means the last time that they would be so radical in their artistic leanings. Their hunger to explore new creative directions would soon lead to something of a dead end for most of the band's members; for one, it would lead to the taking of a momentous, even defining, decision.

5
No Sleep 'til The Exit Door

Interviewed in 2001 during a tour of the USA for which Deep Purple were on a triple bill with Ted Nugent and the glorified tribute act that went out under the name of Lynyrd Skynyrd, Glover promised a new studio album: 'California and the West is really going to be the next step — and then the album will come out. New studio record we'll be making later this year. Can't tell you anything about it because it's not been made yet. It's typically [sic] with us — it's pretty spontaneous.'[1] He stated that the orchestra tour had put back the album writing and recording sessions and 'changed our thinking'.

It may not have been the only thing. That the orchestra tour had been a success was undeniable. Huge crowds had turned out and the 'Concerto' had gone from being an oddity to an integral part of Deep Purple's repertoire. No longer that weird thing from the boring album that no-one listens to, it now existed in numerous recordings (although not yet a studio version) and took its place alongside 'Smoke On The Water', 'Highway Star' and 'Black Night' as a viable setlist entry. It still occupied a unique position, of course, and Glover was right to point out that despite being 'for group and orchestra', it included remarkably little group. Nonetheless, that the tour represented something of a sea change for the band would become increasingly clear moving forward.

Around this time Luciano Pavarotti called. For those who do not know, Pavarotti was one of the greatest tenors to have ever lived. Born into a cash-strapped household in Modena,

Italy, in 1935, his passions were defiantly of the time and place that he lived: football and opera, two activities that have more in common than is often appreciated. Failing to make his way in the former, he turned his attention to the latter. Cursed with a father who saw big risks in trying to be a dreamcatcher, Luciano only began serious study of singing at the age of nineteen, allegedly never learning how to read music — a point of comparison, perhaps, with many rock stars. His career in opera during the seventies and eighties was increasingly stellar; his movie career less so (his film, *Yes, Giorgio*, from 1982, endured a critical mauling and was a catastrophic failure at the box office).

In 1990, two things happened to remove the qualification 'in the opera world' and make him a massive international star, full stop. The first was the BBC's use of him singing his signature aria 'Nessun Dorma' (from Puccini's opera *Turandot*) as the theme for their coverage of the football World Cup, which was being held that year in Italy. Opening titles of sporting events had previously always been functional and unexciting, but, as of *Italia 90*, they began to be treated as minor cultural landmarks in their own right. The single of 'Nessun Dorma' was a chart-busting smash hit on a scale that many a top pop group would envy. Irrespective of Jon Lord's efforts, crossovers of this type were rare, classical musicians not often achieving the sort of rock star status to which Pavarotti was now propelled.

It was cemented by the second key happening of the year — the first 'Three Tenors' concert. Staged on the eve of the World Cup in the evocative surroundings of Rome's Baths of Caracalla, it brought together Pavarotti and the other two tenor superstars, Placido Domingo and Jose Carreras. The concert — together with its follow-up at the World Cup closing ceremony — was another trendsetter in being an early example of classical music presented in a pop style. Now, it is common to see string quartets and the like bashing out Sex Pistols songs, or having some fun as their members try to outdo each other for speed, but, back then, the taking of some of opera's catchier arias and repackaging them as wave-your-lighter-in-the-air anthems was a new idea. The resulting genre has been called 'popera' and 'stadium classical.'[2] The albums that it spawned have sold millions of copies, doubtless to the considerable benefit of The Three Tenors' bank balances and, in the longer term, the careers of such imitators as Andrea Bocelli and Charlotte Church.

Deep Purple entered this glittering picture via a nearly-annual event, 'Pavarotti and Friends'. This was a kind of sentimental homecoming for the singer, as it took place in Modena. He played the part of jovial host, introducing, and performing with, guest stars, the whole shebang being staged to raise money for various charities, including the United Nations High Commission for Refugees. Pavarotti faced criticism over the years for sharing a stage with pop stars, a piece of snobbery he was quick to shoot down: 'Some say the word 'pop' is a derogatory word to say, 'not important' — I do not accept that. If the word 'classic' is the word to say 'boring', I do not accept. There is good and bad music.'[3]

For the 2001 iteration of the concert, an impressive line-up was assembled. Tom Jones, Barry White, George Benson, Anastacia, Bond and Morcheeba were all on the bill, while top-of-the-A-list Hollywood stars Michael Douglas and Catherine Zeta-Jones lent their support, along with the fashion designer and mogul Donatella Versace. Deep Purple's involvement came about, Glover suggested, because Pavarotti had heard them playing with an orchestra and assumed that they were primarily a crossover act.[4] This may have been a misreading of the maestro's attitude towards rock and pop music.

The evening got going in syrupy fashion with a children's choir, before the professionals took centre stage. Morcheeba covered Dean Martin's 'That's Amore', Tom Jones — somewhat inappropriately — gave the crowd 'Sex Bomb', Barry White went for 'Let The Music Play'. Deep Purple contributed two items. Towards the end — just before the all-star singalong of The Beatles' 'With A Little Help From My Friends' — they, predictably, played 'Smoke On The Water'. Before that, however, they joined Pavarotti for a version of nothing less than 'Nessun Dorma'.

Films of the night show a huge crowd flanked by the grand buildings of the Parco Novi Sad. The band are mostly attired in their usual 'no dress code' style as they walk out on to the stage. Gillan wears a white suit. His hair is cropped, the trademark lengthy locks now a fading memory (they have never fully returned). This is him in serious mode.

The potential for falling flat on his face is high, so, understandably, there is a certain nervousness in the air. Interviewed about the piece that he is about to tackle, Gillan said: 'Nessun Dorma' is really a classic rock 'n' roll tune. Obviously not — it's an aria from Puccini's *Turandot*, but, I mean, it's a classic rock tune — it could be. So it came very naturally. There was no way I was going to try to sing it as an opera singer, but, apart from the way in which we sing, which is different, we all project from the diaphragm and we all use our heads and our voice boxes and that sort of thing.'[5]

Gillan sings the song in English and wisely makes no attempt to deviate from his usual style. Why should he? He is, after all, the man who successfully hit the near impossible notes in 'Child In Time' and 'Gethsemene' (from *Jesus Christ Superstar*). His voice melds well with that of Pavarotti, his partner in the duet. In many ways, the performance completes the project begun with the first Three Tenors concert and is an interesting side note to the *Concerto for Group and Orchestra*.

Like that magnum opus, it is a crossover, but, this time, the door is opened by the classical side. Rock is invited in to the elite inner circle of the highest of high art forms and the meeting is unexpectedly harmonious. In a few short minutes,

Gillan confirms the 'cool' status of opera arias. He went on to claim that the performance led to Pavarotti making an extraordinary admission: "'I'm very jealous of you…" He told me, "I'm jealous of you because I've heard you sing 'Smoke on the Water' several times, and in each of them it sounds different. Your expression is slightly different every night that you interpret the song. If I do this with one of my famous arias, I would be crucified by the critics and the audience; they want everything to always sound the same.'"[6]

Deep Purple — and Gillan in particular — formed quite a bond with Pavarotti. They were invited back in 2003 for the final '…and Friends' benefit, at which they shared a bill with, among others, Eric Clapton. Again, the 'Nessun Dorma' duet was a centrepiece.

After Pavarotti's death in 2007, Gillan spoke of how close he had become to the maestro: 'I sang with him twice and got to know him fairly well. He was a regular bloke. He called me at home before the first time we sang, and said: [adopts Italian accent] "So we sing a song together. What shall we sing? Child In Time?" I went: "Thanks, but not really. How about Nessun Dorma?" It went quiet on the phone. And then he went: "Nessun Dorma? You wanna sing Nessun Dorma? With me? You fucking crazy!" He wanted to be a pop star. That was behind everything he thought of. He wanted us to make a record together of covers.'[7] The record never appeared, but a mutual respect, if not affection, remained between the two men. Gillan even admitted to having cried when Pavarotti died.

There was little room for sentimentality in any other area, however, and orchestras, arias and opera singers duly dispensed with, the relentless round of touring continued. Specifically, the triple-header with Nugent and Lynyrd Skynyrd wended its way around North America during the middle of 2001 playing to appreciative audiences for whom Deep Purple were definitely not the main draw. Not everything went according to plan. Nugent dropped out before the end, leaving the others to soldier on without him.

Decamping to Germany, the first eight dates of what was supposed to be Deep Purple's European tour (now supported by Manfred Mann's Earth Band and a collective calling themselves April Daze) were played without Lord, who was forced out because of surgery to his knee. His place at the keyboards was taken by an old trouper named Don Airey.

On the subject of the new studio album, Glover could only say: 'There's a great enthusiasm in the band for making a really, really great album, a spectacularly different album that will be bold. It will be strange, it will be different, but there's nothing much written.'[8] Such news certainly suggested a change in the band's ideas and it can only have been as a result of the Orchestra Tour and other happenings at around the same time. Whatever else the experience had achieved, a point had been proved about the band's capabilities, not to mention ambition. In many ways, Glover's words represent the triumph of Gillan, whose desire to produce something significant and highly produced had lost out to Blackmore's less complicated plan for the disastrous *The Battle Rages On...* project.

Unfortunately, as Glover points out, ambition is one thing, but it remains just that — ambition — without the work to make it happen and not much had been possible. It would be unfair to say that absolutely nothing was happening on that front. Gigs in England in the early months of 2002 included a song called 'Up The Wall' that had come out of recent writing sessions. Complex musically, it would go on to appear more formally under another title. In either guise, it is nowhere near as much fun as 'Long Time Gone'.

Those UK gigs were notable in other ways, too. After only a handful had been played, illness, mainly to Ian Gillan, led to the rest of the tour being cancelled and rescheduled for September. The break gave at least one of them time to reflect

— perhaps too much time.

In March, it was announced that Lord had quit. Sold as a 'retirement', it actually had all the hallmarks of a straightforward resignation. Glover's comment at the time sounded like nothing so much as a press release: 'Jon has told us he plans to retire from active participation in Deep Purple. We wish him the best. The moment cannot pass without a personal comment. It is sad that Jon has come to this difficult decision but every one of us respects his right to determine his own life. I have learned so much from him that I could not possibly do him justice by attempting to quantify it.'[9]

There were many reasons for Lord's decision. One was hinted at by Marco De Goeij: recent adventures had convinced Lord that he could make a success of being a classical composer. The orchestra tour had affirmed this, but *Pictured Within* is not to be underestimated: Lord had enjoyed touring the album briefly in Germany in the middle of 1999. It was very much the direction in which he wanted to go. More practically, Lord had tired of the never-ending touring. It was gruelling and all-consuming.

He said as much: 'It was a combination of the relentless touring schedules and my desire… I knew there was music that had to be written, bouncing around in my head and playing around my music room with pieces of paper and I knew that if I didn't get round to it and start doing something about it, it would never get done. And I didn't want to be a really old man going "I wish I had" so I decided to do something about it.'[10]

According to *The Guardian*[11], he wrote to the management requesting a year off. His letter received a negative response, leaving him no option but to draw a line under his time with the band.

Paul Mann has confirmed that the decision to leave was by no means lightly taken. Lord frequently doubted the wisdom of his move: 'For him to have given up his place in Deep Purple

— that was an enormous thing. It was a very conflicted thing for him and I think there were times when he thought, "Oh my God, what have I done?" But I think he knew he had to do it if he wanted to really find out whether he could do what he thought he could do, which was to be a composer.'[12]

Gillan, pragmatically, described it as a 'relief', saying, 'We were reluctant to press on with [a new album] at the time because Jon Lord's been leaving for five years. I mean, bless him, he's a monument in the band, but that was kind of unsettling. We didn't know whether to include him in the writing as he had his mind on other things.'[13]

To be fair, Lord's own position was not wildly at odds with this: 'I first thought whether I should or shouldn't [leave] around '97/'98. Then we put the thirtieth anniversary of the 'Concerto' together and that was a wonderful experience and then we toured around the world with that, so obviously I wanted to be part of that.'[14]

This was not just any ordinary change of personnel. Lord was a legend and, to many, he was Deep Purple — well, him and Ian Paice. Blackmore had been, too, of course, but his leaving had been acrimonious and had come at a low ebb for the band. It could have been terminal, with the inevitable implosion unmourned, even welcomed, by most fans. Much had changed since then. Morse had brought the smiles and enthusiasm back. Deep Purple had again become an exciting, creative force. Losing Lord would not kill the body, but the soul, or part of it anyway, would be gone forever.

Thus, this time, there were no clashing egos, no bitchy comments in the press, no gaslighting attempts to control the narrative. It was all very amicable, as the Deep Purple Appreciation Society reported: 'Jon Lord has officially retired from the group in order to spend time on a number of other recording projects which Purple's touring schedule wouldn't permit. He has however offered to contribute to the new studio album which will be recorded in August.'[15] The same announcement mentioned that he would potentially return in a guest slot capacity for forthcoming UK shows.

Happily, this did happen. Lord did not play any complete gigs. The plan was for the band as it then was to reach the keys solo slot, for that to play out for a few minutes until the Hammond Organ lead in to 'Perfect Strangers', which, with a dim of the lights, would be when Lord would take over. Lord's wait for his cue was a bittersweet few minutes for him: 'I wasn't sure how it was going to work. I was as nervous as a kitten. I had a dry mouth; I was pacing around backstage. And to stand backstage and to hear the band that I had formed, playing songs that I had helped to write with different people playing was — the most complex of emotions were playing out.'[16]

In the event, it all worked like clockwork and memories of those gigs — reinforced by YouTube clips — underline how moving it was. Lord was about to become a stranger of sorts, perhaps a perfect one, but, for a handful of songs at least, he was still part of the family. When the lights came back up and the crowd realised what had happened, they erupted. 'One of those things welled up in me, you know, that sometimes you can't stop,' Lord said, 'and I just — I was in tears — I had a lump in my throat that I couldn't quite swallow down.'[17]

Jon Lord played his last ever gig with Deep Purple on 19th September 2002 at the Regent Theatre in Ipswich. Afterwards, he stayed up all night with Paul Mann talking about everything — the past and the future, memories and aspirations, opportunities and challenges and, naturally enough, music. They talked a lot about music, much of it yet to be written.

6.
Going Bananas

So who was the keyboardist who stepped aside just before the huge chords that introduce 'Perfect Strangers' resounded around whichever space the band happened to be in? Who was the man who selflessly let someone else take his place and who returned a song or two later to play duets with his predecessor? Of course, it was the same man who had covered when Lord had been forced to drop out to get surgery the previous year — Don Airey.

He was far from a novice, having an enviable career behind him that had involved his playing with some of the greats of rock. In a very real sense, he was already part of the extended Deep Purple family.

Born in Sunderland in 1948, he was more-or-less a contemporary of the members of the core band and, like Morse, held a degree in Music (from the University of Nottingham), as well as a diploma from the Royal Northern College of Music. In other words, he could go toe-to-toe with Lord as a musician, although he had nothing like the 'Concerto' on his CV. Like Lord, he was not necessarily one hundred percent committed to heavy rock: 'I was a great jazz fan,' he has said, 'I wasn't so keen on pop music as such. My father had a very large collection of 78s that he collected when he was a young man, and we had a record player. I used to listen to people like Fats Waller, Fletcher Henderson, and lots of British big bands.'[1] His career began with a short-notice offer to be band leader on a Mediterranean cruise ship. The genre of choice was jazz, but it led to an invitation to join drummer Cozy Powell's band Hammer. From there, he co-founded Coliseum II with Jon Hiseman, featuring guitarist Gary Moore. It should have been huge, but never quite took off.

Still, the association with Powell put Airey into the Deep Purple orbit and he would go on to emulate the drummer by playing in Rainbow and Whitesnake. Indeed, it was Powell who got him into Rainbow, calling him to audition for Blackmore, whose main concern, Airey said, was not with heavy rock at all: 'He said to me, "Do you like Bach?" I said, "Yeah." He gave me a piece of Bach to read, which I kind of knew, but I pretended I'd never seen it before, so he thought I was sight-reading it. We played it together. I forget what piece of Bach it was, but we kind of rocked it up together. And then he said to me, "Do you know Beethoven's Ninth?"'[2]

He went on to provide the keyboards for the two hit Rainbow albums, *Down To Earth* and *Difficult To Cure*. For the latter, he was a co-arranger of the title track, which was based on his audition piece, Beethoven's Ninth. A not-so fun fact is that it was one of the numbers played at the notorious 1993 NEC Deep Purple gig.

For Whitesnake, Airey was part of the ensemble that produced the monster-selling 'frizzy hair metal' masterpiece that was originally just known as *Whitesnake*, but has subsequently tended to be referred to as '1987' (that being the year of its release) — despite that title appearing nowhere on its packaging. A slightly more fun fact is that the man he replaced in Whitesnake was… Jon Lord. He also played on a new version of an older song that had originally featured Lord, 'Here I Go Again', which, in the form of a speeded-up remix (which possibly includes some of Airey's work), became another chart storming classic.

This is, though, just a part of Airey's rock family tree. He played with Black Sabbath (beating Gillan to the punch by several years), Ozzy Osborne, Gary Moore, Judas Priest, Wishbone Ash and Bruce Dickinson. He even lent his talents to eighties-era Jethro Tull. As with Whitesnake, he happened to be around when many of these artists had their greatest successes. Yet, for all that, he was always something of an unknown quantity. Few have served such a long and extensive rock apprenticeship, but he was never a star in the same way as Jon Lord. He was a journeyman, not quite a session player, but clearly gripped by something of that mentality. He is, though, the only member of Deep Purple to have won the Eurovision Song Contest, an achievement he racked up while playing with Katrina and the Waves.

The decision to move more into the spotlight came once his family life permitted it. After heading off on tour with fellow Whitesnake alumni Bernie Marsden and Mickey Moody as part of a band called Company of Snakes, the call came to stand in for Lord with Deep Purple, initially for three gigs starting two days' later. Three became sixteen, then the tour's full twenty-four. There seemed little reason to believe that he was anything other than a temporary member of the band, although he reported a significant conversation that took place on the road: 'I just had a great time for six weeks while Jon's ill — that's all they said to me. I mean, Gillan sidled up at one point and said, "Er… can I have a word: you know, if Jon doesn't come back…" I said, "Jon's coming back…" I thought Jon would be out of his mind to leave a band like that; I just couldn't see how he could.'[3]

Airey confessed to self-doubt about whether he was up to the job. He need not have worried: 'Bruce [Payne] phoned me up. He said, "Jon's gone, actually. We've got a short list — it's got four names on it." I said, "Oh." He said, "All of them are yours" — which is about the nicest thing anybody's ever said to me.'[4]

Airey's accession to the band, then, was not quite the same

as Morse's. While the 'short list' charade was again indulged in, it was no longer strictly necessary. Airey was the sitting tenant — and how many keyboardists capable of filling Lord's shoes were there, anyway? Morse stepped in when Satriani couldn't. There were no such false starts with Airey. He simply carried on doing what he was already doing, with the only break being for Lord's farewell gigs.

As with Morse, it was never stipulated that Airey be a carbon copy of the person he replaced. He has spoken of the differences between himself and Lord, saying, with characteristic modesty, that he is not on the same level. His given reason is that Lord found a way to play Hammond organ differently from how it had been played in the past, that he forged his own musical identity. Airey, by contrast, was, as he himself saw it, more conventional — standing on the shoulders of giants, not a giant in his own right. He was too self-critical.

While there is justice in the claim that Lord was a unique talent, Airey is still an outstanding musician who inspires nothing but confidence in any audience. If he is behind the keyboards, then it does not matter much what anyone else on stage is doing: the show will go on. Moreover, his main strength is precisely that he is not Lord. Lord's best work sounds symphonic, grand, classical. Airey is all about jazz and there is a swing and a freeform quality to his playing that is distinctively his own — listen to the keyboard solo sections of Deep Purple live albums featuring the two players and you will have no difficulty in telling them apart. As Airey became more embedded in the band, the keyboards became increasingly prominent. In part, this reflected the ways in which the band's sound was evolving, but it also speaks to Airey's ability to place the keyboard at the heart of the music, not only driving it, but leading it.

One consequence of the new line up — Mark X! — getting together was that new album plans were pushed back again. Gigs in the UK may have been postponed, but the rest of the world was still hungry for entertainment and the punishing schedule of tours — Lord's chief bugbear — showed no signs of letting up. Visits to India, Russia and South East Asia were only the prelude to a long spell in North America. August came around, but instead of the promised writing and recording, the band skipped from Los Angeles to Germany for several engagements there, then the delayed UK gigs, then Dubai, then Greece... If Airey had been looking forward to a quiet life with Deep Purple, he certainly did not get it.

Set lists from around this time were unusually adventurous. Not only did 'Fools' continue to hold its place, but a new Dixie Dregs- style instrumental, written by Morse, 'The Well Dressed Guitar' was being honed, 'Up The Wall' was still there, 'The Aviator' reemerged from ill-deserved obscurity and 'Mary Long' (from the *Who Do We Think We Are* album) was added. The last of these is a deep cut gem, musically quite simple, but graced with one of Gillan's best ever lyrics: replete with satire and word play, it is a blatant attack on the kind of moralistic censors who sought to limit what people could consume in the name of entertainment. A typical verse is:

> 'When the nation knew you had children,
> it came as such a surprise;
> We really didn't know you'd had it in you —
> how you did it, we can only surmise'.

Another often included rarity was 'I'm Alone'. Originally the B-side of the 'Strange Kind of Woman' single, it had languished on various compilations until it appeared on the deluxe package that was the *Fireball* anniversary edition. Playing it was a nice experiment, but it was no 'When A Blindman Cries' and was quickly dropped. As a song, it sounds more like something from the band's Mark I line-up than anything the Gillan and Glover era might produce.

Such attempts to refresh the live show were all well and good, but, as for new recordings, it was now over four years since *Abandon* — unacceptably long, in the eyes of many fans. Three new pieces existed — 'Long Time Gone', which, by now, was living up to its name, as well as 'Up The Wall' and 'The Well Dressed Guitar'. Clearly, a new studio collection was overdue.

Glover, in the interview previously quoted, had made a brace of promises: that the album would be epic and that he would not be producing it. The second of these was more consequential than it may have seemed. Deep Purple had always been a self-produced band. Or, rather, they had been produced by Glover (who had also provided similar services for others, such as Judas Priest and Nazareth). The rock stalwart Martin Birch had been involved in the early seventies, but as an engineer, not a producer. His job had been to make sure that things sounded good. He was a techie. Creative, yes, but not in an artistic way.

So what does a music producer do? Put simply, he or she is required to have 'good ears', a rather disingenuous-sounding term that has been defined as: 'the ability to identify, rate, and modify the different parameters of music performance, composition, and arrangement, as well as sound quality (including the acoustics of the instruments, the room, and audio settings).'[5]

Even this comprehensive list does not entirely encapsulate the influence that a producer can have. George Martin's contributions to The Beatles' recordings, for example, were nothing less than momentous. He had as much to do with their sound as anyone else. Indeed, compare what Martin did with 'Sergeant Pepper' to Phil Spector's work on *Let It Be* and the role of a producer should be immediately obvious.

The man who got the job for the new Deep Purple album was Michael Bradford, who, by his own admission, was a longtime, indeed lifelong, fan. Hailing from a working-class area of Detroit, he had previously been associated with an impressive roster of artists, including Madonna and Kid Rock — for whom he was an early advocate. He was also a fine musician who had played in a number of bands.

As he describes it, his connection to Deep Purple initially came through a third party: 'We had the same music publisher in Europe. I had a song that was a big hit in Europe at the time, and the publisher thought that perhaps a producer who was also a songwriter could help Deep Purple with getting their ideas organised. That person sort of acted as a 'matchmaker' between the band and me. Then, I called Bruce Payne, Deep Purple's manager, on the phone, and we set up a meeting in England.'[6]

The 'matchmaker' was Brian Rawlings, an executive with Disney Music. Bradford went to see the band live in Brighton. His chief concerns echoed those of Morse prior to his joining — were the band serious? Did they want to make good, original music and have a hit record? The gig was a partial 'yes' to those questions; meeting the band confirmed it. Bradford was keen to get involved.

Bringing in a producer was a profound change to the band's creative process. It was the introduction of a new voice, a new partner. In some respects, it was an admission of failure: something wasn't quite working that could only be put right with fresh thinking and a different perspective. Morse certainly saw it this way: 'With Michael, he'll go ahead, listen to the versions and be polite, but he'll eventually say no, this is the way it should go and everybody wants that after so many albums of committee.'[7]

This was as much as to say that the hoped-for epic was beyond the scope of the current set-up. Credits for writers from outside the band were not unknown, with both *Slaves and Masters* and *Come Taste The Band* including tracks for which members of the band were only credited as co-writers. There had been good reasons for these. Somebody coming in from the start with a specific remit to share in the creative process had not been done before.

Recording took place during January and February 2003 in Los Angeles. The first month was spent in rehearsals, in order, Bradford said, 'to analyse each song and get them in shape without the pressure of an expensive studio.'[8]

The recording sessions went smoothly, by all accounts, although Morse spoke of the producer introducing a new type of autocracy that had not been present before: 'Michael said, 'No, I want to do a more commercial tune and I'm going to bring it in and you guys are going to make it sound like you' and change the guitar riffs or whatever.'[9]

Even so, Glover spoke of his 'pure joy' at working with such a top producer, concluding, in characteristic style: 'We have a title, which I cannot divulge — I can't even tell you what it's called. Until they are mixed no decisions have been made regarding what goes on the album or what's included out, if and when, or at all. Michael Bradford did some writing with us, and he engineered the recording as well as produced. He's very good with menus. There is no rapping and we don't sound like Kid Rock. No Balinese drummers. It will be released sometime late August /early September — as far as any fule kno.'[10]

The title was revealed by Gillan during a gig early in the year — 'Bananas'. There were plenty of fans who thought that this was provisional, or temporary, or just another example of Gillan's stage banter. It was soon enough confirmed that it was none of those things: it was the title.

Its provenance was explained by Glover in an interview: 'About three years ago, we were on a tour of Australia; it was a Sunday; we'd had a long flight, I think from somewhere to Perth, about a five-hour flight. And we were sitting there and I've got all the Sunday papers with supplements and Ian Gillan's sitting next to me in the window seat doing the crossword. And I'm reading the papers and I came across the Travel section and there was a photograph there of — it was a Vietnamese travel story — and there was a photograph of a guy pushing a bike with great difficulty because on the front of the bike is an enormous mound of bananas. It's a lovely photograph and I looked at it and I said to Ian, I said, "Look, there's an album cover. Just use the photograph and call it *Bananas*." He said, "Brilliant!" I said, "No, no. I was joking.'"[11]

That conversation was neither taken as a joke nor forgotten. When the album was released in August, that was more-or-less precisely what the fans got. The one main change was that the photograph in question was relegated to the back cover; a similar picture of a guy sitting on top of a large pile of bananas was used for the front. It was a very simple design that was a far cry from the slickness of *Abandon*, despite EMI again being the label behind it.

Much enthusiasm and bullish talk propelled the album into the shops and the relatively new world of online stores. Reviews were reasonably positive. Nonetheless, *Bananas* has not weathered well and is now often rated as one of the band's worst efforts. What could have gone wrong?

It was certainly not a lack of input from talented people. Two songs — 'I Got Your Number', which is an evolution of 'Up The Wall', and 'Picture of Innocence' — dated from the Jon Lord days and he is credited as co-writer on both. Bradford explained how they were dealt with in the studio: 'Those two songs started as demos that they had recorded before I was involved. In rehearsal, we worked on the arrangements and streamlined them some more. Then we re-recorded them at Royaltone [studio]. They were pretty heavily re-arranged to make them flow better.'[12]

On two other songs — the opener 'House Of Pain', and 'Walk On' — the only credited writers are Bradford and Gillan. Morse is sole author of the album's final track, a brief instrumental titled 'Contact Lost', which was written to commemorate the loss of the Space Shuttle Columbia, a tragedy that occurred contemporaneously with the recording sessions. Morse was moved to write the piece upon hearing that Kalpana Chawla, one of the astronauts, had taken a couple of Deep Purple CDs, including *Purpendicular*, on board with her.

Unfortunately, none of this succeeded in producing the type of work that Glover had been predicting — and promising. A major issue was the inclusion on the song 'Haunted' of female backing vocals (supplied by Beth Hart) and a string section. These elements have appeared on more recent albums without controversy — strings had been included before — but, on 'Haunted', they were criticised by many as 'not Deep Purple'. It probably does not help that the song is a rather middle-of-the-road ballad that could be by any of a dozen soft rock bands.

Bradford's take is intriguing: "Haunted' is actually a throwback to a more 60s British soul music sound. It is probably more akin to Procol Harum or Spencer Davis or Traffic than anything going on today. They were not really worried about formula because they have been together for so long and they have made many albums.'[13]

This may be a reminder that Deep Purple have never been an easily pigeonholed band, but it fails to disguise the main problem with the album: the songs are just not that great.

'House Of Pain' is perhaps most representative of Deep Purple's usual output. It is heavy and rocky and begins with a classic Gillan scream. It has a simple riff and something of a bar room chorus that are not unentertaining, but the band are clearly having more fun than their listeners are likely to. In all honesty, the track is like something that was knocked out in ten minutes of spare studio time when someone realised that the album lacked a barnstorming opener.

From there, it is one competent, but unmemorable, track

after another. Nothing is certifiably terrible, but nothing really stands out either. 'Walk On' is a moody blues tune, 'Sun Goes Down' is ho-hum heavy and 'Bananas' is, well, a bit bananas. 'I Got Your Number' is not as effective as 'Up The Wall', its offbeat riff being more annoying than enjoyable. The news is not all bad. 'Contact Lost' is gorgeous, although it is to be regretted that its inclusion meant that the other available instrumental — 'The Well Dressed Guitar' — was left off.

'Silver Tongue' served as a powerful gig opener for a while. In hindsight, the best of the bunch (pun intended) is a track that was widely criticised by fans upon first hearing, but has stood the test of time unexpectedly well, 'Razzle Dazzle'. For nearly two decades, it was — bafflingly — Gillan's favourite Deep Purple song. His opinion is surely not shared by many, but the song has a bouncy, party-style, riff and a fun lyric (recounting the carnage that ensues from a night out 'on the raz') that at least put a smile on the face.

In some ways, it is sad that the album is not a better piece of work. It is, after all, the crossover point between keyboard players, neither of whom it serves well. For Lord, it represents the last time that he contributed anything to Deep Purple creatively — not the best of legacies. For Airey, it left things still to prove.

In looking for culprits, it would be easy to blame Bradford, especially as he refused to step back, insisting on an active role in the writing. That would be unfair. Glover's comments ahead of the album's release provide more of a clue: they simply tried too hard. Bringing in a producer was not a bad idea — they have never since gone back — and Bradford can be credited with taking the band in new directions that they have continued to explore. But, with so many changes happening all at once, something more in the band's comfort zone might have been the wiser way to go.

Bananas was released on 25th August 2003. Dependably,

German and Finnish people bought it in sufficient quantities for it to register in the higher reaches of those countries' charts. Everywhere else, it struggled. To date, it has sold around 250,000 copies worldwide — the downward trend continued.

7
Enraptured

On 23rd September 2003 at a gig in Mexico City, Deep Purple were presented with the remains of the CDs that Kalpana Chawla had taken with her on the ill-fated last flight of the space shuttle Columbia. They were handed over by her husband Jean-Pierre Harrison. Certificates of authenticity from NASA were included in the package. If Deep Purple needed any confirmation of the esteem in which they were held — album sales notwithstanding — then that was it.

A nice and moving touch, the presentation was a moment out of a year largely spent promoting *Bananas*. This continued into 2004 in a relentless round of gigs that took in just about everywhere. A reunion with Joe Satriani — who filled the support act slot — happened during dates in the USA. Otherwise, days and nights on the road must have blurred into each other. It is legitimate to ask whether the band were doing anything special, or whether being on tour was now just a full-time job.

With Deep Purple in something of a groove — or perhaps holding pattern — other projects were given some space to move forward. Some were just pie in the sky and were destined to remain so. Glover planned to bring back *The Butterfly Ball* for a one-off performance at the Royal Albert Hall (sound familiar?) He also talked about publishing an autobiography. As of this writing, neither has happened, although a report in 2020 said that Glover had made progress on the book.[1]

Rather more productive was a project called Living Loud, which featured Morse and Airey, joined by Bob Daisley (who had been in many of the bands that had included Airey, although not always at the same time), Lee Kerslake (best known for his work with Uriah Heep) and vocalist Jimmy Barnes (who was mostly a solo artist). An album was recorded which — for complex legal reasons — mingled reworkings of Ozzy Osborne songs with new compositions. A single, 'In The Name of God' was released and promptly used as a promotional device by UNICEF.

Morse was very enthusiastic about the project and touted it as being a way to improve his work with Deep Purple: 'The fact that it's something occasional fits right in with Deep Purple very well because everyone in the band does that, and it's encouraged and everyone says it makes a stronger band because the musicians are stronger.'[2]

The album is something of a minor triumph. The Ozzy remakes are what they are, but the originals are funky and bluesy and a whole lotta fun. Squint and songs like 'Last Chance' could be AC/DC heading towards their top gear — which is perhaps to be expected, given how many members of the band were Australian. A piece like 'Every Moment A Lifetime', by contrast, is quieter, more melodic.

Morse was keen to take the music on tour, but, with the exception of a date or two in Sydney, his wish was left unfulfilled. Neither has a follow-up been made. One would certainly be welcome, but with most of the personnel either retired, or, in the case of Kerslake, no longer with us, that is not going to happen.

Back in the main band, an anniversary was coming around — not that of the release of an old classic, but of the start of a career, specifically, Gillan's career. It struck someone that the singer had been plying his trade for forty years and this merited some kind of commemoration. A memoir or autobiography would have been the obvious choice, but Gillan's manager was more interested in producing an album.

As Gillan explained: 'I thought he meant a compilation album of tracks which was the idea I think to start with. I burned a few CDs from my media files and listened to them in the car for a few days and realised it wasn't going to work. The sounds were so different from different eras.'[3] This was especially the case for recordings from Gillan's pre-Purple days with Episode Six and The Javelins.

The idea began to form that the album could consist of remakes of songs. Then another idea formed that it could become a bit of a party, with Gillan's friends and colleagues providing the musical backing. He made some calls. Joe Elliot from Def Leppard joined without hesitation, as did Satriani, Lord, everyone from Purple and Tony Iommi from Black Sabbath. Janick Gers, who, in the dim and distant past, had been the guitarist with the band Gillan, also came along for the ride, as did too many others to mention by name.

The recordings were not all done in the same place at the same time. With the musicians scattered around the world, it was expedient to record in studios in different countries and for some parts to be recorded on top of tracks that already existed. This happened, for example, with Ian Paice's contributions, which were all laid down in one day, with him playing along to the songs for which they were destined.

The relaxed way in which it was recorded is reflected in the finished album. Most of the tracks are heavy and it is obvious that everyone involved is having a good time playing them. The choice of songs is interesting, although it would be a mistake to read too much into it as far as Gillan's own preferences are concerned.

Iommi's presence meant that something from the Black Sabbath period was needed, so 'Trashed' was included. Gers' time in the band Gillan was covered by 'Bluesy Blue Sea' and so on. It is perhaps strange that *Dreamcatcher* is represented twice — by 'A Day Late...' and 'Sugar Plum' — even more so in that Steve Morris is the guitarist for neither. 'No Worries' is a new song and a pleasantly enjoyable one at that. The selections from Deep Purple's catalogue are more-or less what might be expected. 'Smoke On The Water' — obviously — 'When A Blindman Cries' (played by the actually blind Jeff Healey — a coincidence that only occurred to everyone involved after the fact) and 'Speed King'. A 'deluxe tour edition' that followed after a respectable interval, added 'Demon's Eye' and a live take on the blues piece 'Wasted Sunsets'.

The book idea was not completely dropped, since *Gillan's Inn* was a dual disc. On one side was the CD and on the other, a DVD of extra bits: handwritten lyrics, Gillan's introductions to the songs, 'Demon's Eye' initially, some films. There was also a feature that allowed listeners to change the lead guitarist on 'Smoke On The Water' to hear a range of interpretations of the immortal riff.

It was all nice to have, but not very essential. Cutting edge at the time, the growth of YouTube and the fading away of DVD players have left it feeling a bit quaint. It is to be wondered how often buyers of the package ever played the DVD side.

A bit of trivia concerns the manufacturing of the tour edition (which did not come out until 2007). A mistake at the factory meant that some early editions lacked some of the added 'bonus tracks' and went out instead with a cover version of Marvin Gaye's 'Can I Get A Witness?' Now collector's items, they were replaced for free by the record company: their lucky owners thus got a copy of the album and a valuable rarity for their money.

Overall, *Gillan's Inn* is entertaining with well-chosen content, although whether it is an apt way to celebrate a forty-year career in showbiz is a moot point. Gillan denied that the new versions of songs would ever replace the originals, but this is also up for discussion in some cases. The rockier take on the *Dreamcatcher* material beats hands down the whimsical and folky direction opted for first time around. Similarly, some of the Gillan band songs benefit from their make overs.

In the end, the best thing that can be said about *Gillian's Inn* is that it is a rare coming together of so many great talents from the rock world. There is something quite thrilling about hearing Jeff Healey and Jon Lord play together, or Tony Iommi, Ian Paice and Roger Glover. Such combinations would have been, at best, unlikely in any other context. In that some of those involved have since passed on, the album has achieved the status of historical document.

Although it was recorded in 2005, *Gillan's Inn* came out in April 2006. It hardly dented the charts. Even the Finns and Germans largely eschewed it. Still, it remains an intriguing moment in time and is definitely worth seeking out for those who have not done so already.

As the availability of a 'tour edition' indicates, Gillan went briefly on the road with the album in late 2006. A gig at the House of Blues in Anaheim, California, on 14th September was recorded and released in 2008. A thoroughly enjoyable set, it features most of the songs from *Gillan's Inn* played by a band that included Michael Lee Jackson on guitar and Joe Mennonna on keyboards, saxophones and backing vocals. That other Michael, Bradford, pops up to guest on a couple of songs. When introducing Jackson's 'Texas State Of Mind' — which is not on *Gillan's Inn* — the singer announces that he is so taken with the song that he has every intention of stealing it. It was a promise that he was to make good...

A less auspicious celebration of Gillan's career was a DVD containing a very long documentary that went under the title, *Highway Star: A Journey in Rock*. Again, friends and colleagues came together to praise the main man, who, for some reason chose to be interviewed in a rowing boat. The DVD included little that was not already known, although Pavarotti did pop up to laud his sometime singing partner's 'genius.' The DVD is listed on Amazon as 'currently unavailable'.

Back in Deep Purple, thoughts were beginning to turn to a new album. *Bananas* may have been talked up by everyone, but it had not been the anticipated chef d'oeuvre and it was already disappearing from the live set. The same approach would not be taken this time.

For a start, the releasing label changed again. Moving on from EMI, the band took up with the German company Edel. It can only be assumed that commercial reasons were behind this move; Gillan hinted as much in a letter: 'Deep Purple sold around 150,000 tickets in the UK alone, at the beginning and end of the 'Bananas' tour that covered about 38 countries in 18 months and played to millions around the world. EMI in the UK pressed — and sold easily — 18,000 copies. They refused point blank to produce any more. Enough, we move on. DP is no longer with EMI.'[4]

Bradford's role this time was drastically different from what it had been. Far less front and centre, it is easy to forget that he actually produced what was finally released. He is not credited as writer on any of the songs and the emphasis in all of the pre-publicity was on how 'spontaneous' the process of making it was: this time, long rehearsal periods were out!

Glover, interviewed around its release had this to say: 'Sometimes you have a writing session, where you write the songs, then you have a recording session, when you record them. This album was done pretty much at the same time: we'd go in, write what was going to be the idea for the song and immediately go into record mode and captured it. Michael is very good at stopping us from overdoing it. Usually, it's two takes and that's it!'[5]

Airey took a similar view, emphasising the difference in sound from *Bananas*: 'It's a bit of a departure from the last album. It's a lot heavier, and I think it will turn a few heads. We recorded it in the same studio that used to be used by Korn and it's got a wonderful sound. It's got a real, immediate drum and organ sound. I was really happy working in there.'[6]

The subtext is clear. Slick production, overdubs, backing vocals and other musicians were not on the agenda: this was to be the band, doing what they do, developing everything from jams and laying it down with as much of a live feel as possible. Another theme is a disregard of — even contempt for — commerciality. Gillan spoke of the merit of longer songs, while Glover — somewhat disingenuously — described Deep Purple as an 'underground band.'[7]

Paice decried the tendency of media outlets to concentrate only on music by currently fashionable artists, meaning that any attempt to produce a radio-friendly' single was futile for a band like Deep Purple.[8]

The album was in the can by June of 2005. Before it could be released, the band found themselves on the bill for Live 8, playing Barrie Park in Ontario, Canada in front of a live TV audience.

A controversial series of concerts organised by the redoubtable Bob Geldof and timed to coincide with a G8 summit in Scotland, Live 8 also marked twenty years since the cultural landmark that had been Live Aid. It was not, however, intended to be 'Live Aid 2', having a more ambitious goal than simply to raise funds to combat a single humanitarian disaster.

On this occasion, the participants were playing to make poverty in Africa a thing of the past and to bring about justice for everyone everywhere — or something like that. Without a specific focus, it was hard to get too excited about and has faded from the memory in a way that its illustrious predecessor never has.

Ten concerts were held in the G8 countries and South Africa on 2nd July. Regardless of musical quality or ideological direction, the mind-boggling logistical feat that this represents is worthy of admiration. The collection of performers at some of the concerts was undeniably sensational. In London, the big news was that Pink Floyd's classic line-up got back together to contribute a short set. They were programmed alongside the likes of Sting, Paul McCartney, Madonna and U2. A-listers such as Brad Pitt, Will Smith and, of all people, Bill Gates, turned up merely to show their faces and do a bit of introducing.

The Canada branch of the franchise was not exactly lacking in star power either. Mötley Crüe, Celine Dion and Neil Young all made appearances, with Dan Aykroyd as compère. Deep Purple played 'Smoke On The Water', Highway Star' and 'Hush', a trinity that would be repeated at a different special event over a decade later.

Despite everything, criticisms were thrown at Live 8 and its organisers. The fact that few performers of African origin were involved was described as patronising — at best. A putative one-off reunion of the Spice Girls never happened and Oasis declined their invitation on the grounds that they did not believe that rock stars could make a meaningful difference to anything. Indeed, many commentators berated the event for making the chief beneficiaries the artists themselves — who, it was suggested, were gifted a golden opportunity to resuscitate careers on the wane (although how much those named above needed such a boost is highly debatable).

This was particularly the case with the Ontario concert, which was generally mocked as being populated by has-beens. That may have been, but it rather overlooks the fact that the original Live Aid had featured plenty of here-today-gone-tomorrow eighties acts (Howard Jones, anyone?) Perhaps it is better to be a has-been than an only-just-was.

Interviewed after the band's slot by Canadian television, Gillan toed the party line, emphasising the purpose of the concerts: 'The message is be loud. As far as the whole issue of this, the whole issue of Africa is concerned, we need to be very loud, so — yeah, that's not a bad thing.'[9]

Due to play a gig later that day, the band reinforced the 'make poverty history' message by taking a private jet to the venue in Illinois.

The new album — *Rapture Of The Deep* — was released on 24th October 2005. The title is a phrase coined, supposedly, by famous diver Jacques Cousteau and refers to a mental state that can be reached when swimming at depths of thirty metres or more. In the context of the album, it was explained by various members of the band as being a feeling of euphoria combined with a sense of danger.[10] This was connected to both the style of music and the way in which it had been written and recorded. It was, moreover, something of a theme of the album. The lyrics are no longer the load of rubbish that afflicted so many of the tracks on *Abandon* and its ilk.

Now — however opaque they are in places — the lyrics mean something. The major preoccupation of several of them is spiritual experience. This is especially true of the title track. A song that could not have been made by any band built in the image of Ritchie Blackmore, it is a six-minute blast of strong, vaguely Eastern sounding, riffs, wistful solos and mystical poetry. The title is only mentioned once, in a beguiling line towards the end:

'But it's alright,
We walk in our sleep.
Yes, it's alright,
This is rapture of the deep'

Other tracks that explore similar territory are the standouts 'Clearly Quite Absurd' and the Doors-y 'Before Time Began.'

It's not all New Age hokum. Familiar ideas are returned to in 'Wrong Man', 'Girls Like That' and 'Money Talks'. 'Back To Back' is an entertaining discussion of sex. It begins by stating that the narrator has read that 'the average man' gets an erection five times a day, something that has been proven because, 'they asked the average man in a survey across the nation'. What sort of sexual satisfaction can be achieved 'back to back' is left unstated.

'Junkyard Blues' is a nice reminder of how rich the band's basic palette can be. Gillan put it into a broader context: 'I was talking to a friend of mine who said, 'White guys can't play the blues, or they shouldn't play the blues — what right do they have to play the blues?' And I said, 'Listen — I have heard a lot of blues records and they're not all about slavery and those sorts of things! There's an awful lot of blues songs about drinking and women' and I told my black friend, 'There's lots of simple things in the blues.''[11]

The most satirical song is 'MTV', which more-or-less restates the band's complaints about their lack of airplay. Of it, Gillan said: 'It's really about classic rock radio. I came to the conclusion that more traffic accidents are caused by classic rock radio than by drink driving — because people are falling asleep at the wheel through total boredom because they play the same old songs over and over again.'[12] He went on to recount a story of Glover being interviewed about a new album only for every question to be about 'Smoke On The Water': this incident is referenced directly in the lyrics.

For all that, *Rapture Of The Deep* is only a slight improvement on *Bananas*. The songs are generally more entertaining, but nothing screams 'future classic'. 'Before Time Began' is the one on which the band tried the hardest, but that has gained next to no traction in the consciousness of fans.

The title track graced set lists for a few years, but nothing else really had much life beyond the album, apart, oddly, from 'Things I Never Said' which was included as a bonus on the album's Japanese release.

Essentially, it comes down to most of the things that the band said about the album at the time of its release being nonsense. It is not particularly heavy — it is far less so than *Abandon* and does not come close in this department to what the band were doing in the early seventies.

This is evident from the cover, if nowhere else: a rather whimsical cartoon of a man wobbling as though reflected in water, while his actual reflection is perfectly still, is offset by curly fonts and a pastel pink background. It is fine as far as it goes, but it does not promise headbanging music.

Of that, the sound is actually quite — whisper it! — commercial. It may have been claimed that everything was thrown together in the studio in an unplanned frenzy of creativity and brio, but it does not come across that way. It has obviously been produced to within an inch of its life and aimed fairly and squarely at the soft rock market.

As with *Gillan's Inn*, an expanded version came out some time later. The most noticeable feature of this was that the pink of the cover had been replaced by a (supposedly) butcher blue. The highlights of the contents were a long overdue studio take on 'The Well Dressed Guitar' (which was by now an established part of the live set) and, for the benefit of anyone outside Japan, 'Things I Never Said'.

Critics were generally impressed, the BBC, for example, stating: 'Don Airey is the star of the show, returning the trademark Hammond sound to the band from whence it came, whilst forming a chemistry with guitarist Steve Morse that was largely missing on their last album', adding, 'This is classic Deep Purple. Welcome back.'[13]

In the full glare of hindsight, this comes across as a massive overstatement. *Rapture Of The Deep* is good, but 'classic Deep Purple'? Not a chance. Airey and Morse do, for certain, perform well together, but not so much as to make the listener forget that this was the second Deep Purple album for one, the fourth for the other and none — with the possible exception of *Purpendicular* — could hold its own with the band's output from the early seventies, or even the mid-eighties.

Well, perhaps they would do better next time. Perhaps. Except that that 'next time' was not to come for a very long time and, for a very long time, looked like it would never come at all.

Real Drum & Bass music. Open Air Festival, Muehldorf am Inn, Bavaria, Germany, 13th June 2009.

(Heiner Heine / Broker.com GmbH & Co. KG / Alamy Stock Photo)

A rare sight. Deep Purple did nine shows with Ex-Jamiroquai bassist Nick Fyffe, while Roger was in Switzerland where his girlfriend was giving birth to their daughter.
This shot is from Eleftheria Arena, Nicosia, Cyprus, 8th May 2011.

(Michalis Ppalis - Editorial / Alamy Stock Photo)

Roger is back for the North American tour. Bethel Woods Centre for the Arts in New York, 12th June 2011.
(Kevin Ferguson / AFF / Alamy Stock Photo)

The Prince of Wales (now King Charles III) during a pre-concert reception prior to the Sunflower Jam Concert at the Royal Albert Hall on 8th July 2011 — a musical event developed in 2006 by Ian Paice's wife Jacky to raise money for people who will benefit from what complementary therapies have to offer.
Top: With Jacky Paice, Don Airey and Roger Glover.
Below: Comedian, Bill Bailey, Jacky Paice, Don Airey, Roger Glover, Steve Morse and Ian Gillan. The latter enjoying a laugh with His Royal Highness.
(Yui Mok / Press Association / Alamy Stock Photo)

Over the years Deep Purple have become synonymous with the Montreux Jazz Festival, with several of their performances recorded and commercially released. Here they are on 16th July 2011 where the songs were enhanced with orchestral accompaniment.
(Loona / Abaca Press / Alamy Stock Photo)

Don during the soundcheck prior to the concert with the symphony orchestra Neue Philharmonie Frankfurt in Dresden, 23rd July 2011.
(Lutz Mueller-Bohlen / dpa picture alliance archive / Alamy Stock Photo)

Steve Morse with the American guitarist Gretchen Menn at the Jason Becker benefit in San Francisco, California 24th January 2013.
(Ross Pelton / MediaPunch Inc / Alamy Stock Photo)

Morse performing at the G3 concert in Prague, Czech Republic, 31st July 2012.
(Michal Dolezal / CTK / Alamy Stock Photo)

At the AWD-Arena in Hanover, Germany, 17th November 2012. The band was presented with hold Hannover 96 shirts before the Bundesliga match against SC Freiburg.
(Carmen Jaspersen / dpa picture alliance archive / Alamy Stock Photo)

Heineken Music Hall, Amsterdam, 4th December 2012. 4th December is hugely significant in Purple folklore. On that date in 1971 the Montreux Casino burnt down. In 1975 the Tommy Bolin line-up played the ill-fated concert in Jakarta and the following year Bolin died on 4th December. Interestingly Deep Purple didn't play a gig on the 4th December again until Le Cube Parc des Expos, Troyes, France in 2010. This gig in Amsterdam was only the second on 4th December since Jakarta.
(WENN Rights Ltd / Alamy Stock Photo)

Gillan during 'No One Came' at the Entertainment Centre in Brisbane, 26th February 2013.
(Dave Hunt / Australian Associated Press / Alamy Stock Photo)

Filming for the video for 'Vincent Price' at the Berlin Dungeon, 27th April 2013.
(Britta Pedersen /dpa picture alliance / Alamy Stock Photo)

Roger and Paicey during the press conference for the Open Air Concert on the Idalp in Ischgl, Austria, 30th April 2013.
(Felix Hörhager / dpa picture alliance / Alamy Stock Photo)

Celebrating Jon Lord concert at Royal Albert Hall, 4th April 2014.
(WENN Rights Ltd / Alamy Stock Photo)

8
To Russia With Rock

The founder and chief curator of the Montreux Jazz Festival, 'Funky Claude' Nobs — who has forever been immortalised in the lyrics to 'Smoke On The Water' — announced that Deep Purple would be playing the event again in 2006.

Whatever words he used were widely interpreted as a suggestion that Blackmore and Lord might be joining the band on stage for a one-off reunion. Glover was quick to issue a denial: 'We are NOT looking for Ritchie (or Jon for that matter) to join us in Montreux. We have contacted our friend Claude Nobs to find out what he was thinking of and he has told us that he didn't say that. He claims he was misquoted. As a rumour mill, the Internet is beyond par; I am still being asked about 'Jon Lord's Dream', a complete non-story if ever there was one.'[1]

Lord's 'dream' was his often-referenced desire for all living members of Deep Purple to play together, at least once. In fact, this is something else that was never said in precisely the way that it was taken. It seems to have originated as a throwaway comment made during a radio interview on Total Rock Radio with Malcolm Dome, as Lord attempted to clarify: 'Yeah, I said that was my dream. It was then picked up and touted as my intent as something I was going to try and put together, which was nothing of the sort. I just thought it would be a wonderful idea. I doubt very much if it would be possible.'[2]

That this palpable nonsense was allowed to take root and grow speaks to two linked trends that were becoming more significant at the time and which Glover's rather frustrated-sounding message acknowledged: the growth of the Internet as the world's chief medium of communication and the increasing factionalism and polarisation of fan bases, Deep Purple's being no exception.

The first is really the subtext to Deep Purple's history during the period covered by this book. The Internet barely registered in 1993. Blackmore could disrupt a gig by throwing water over someone and, unless you were there, you were unlikely to find out about it. Now, it would be filmed on a phone camera and posted on Instagram almost immediately — it is 'insta' gram, after all. Indeed, the incident became news again many years later only after the Internet had taken it up and run with it.

The band have never been averse to making use of the technology for their own benefit, of course. Fan sites, such as *The Highway Star* and the *Deep Purple Appreciation Society* web page have existed for what is now decades. An official site can also be accessed. That is not to mention the websites operated by, and on behalf of, the band's individual members (Gillan's *Caramba* being one example).

It may not have gone unnoticed that 'electronic press kits' have been quoted for most of the albums so far covered by this book. Write about the Deep Purple of the early seventies and your chief sources are *Melody Maker*, *New Musical Express* and similar; write about the band as it is today, and your reference list will be full of hypertext links that can helpfully be clicked on and accessed in the e-version of the published book.

Nancy Baym[3] has argued that the Internet has enabled music fans to evolve from an amorphous mass of consumers to active networked participants in the music industry. The relationship between performers and their fans has changed, become more intimate. So, too, has the purpose of live performance and the releasing of studio recorded music. Gillan has bemoaned the fact that playing a new song at a gig these days is equivalent to putting it out officially because it is in the pocket of every fan, seconds after the last note has quivered to silence.

For Deep Purple in 2006 — and subsequently — the Internet created a schism among fans (the second of the themes mentioned above) that has never really gone away. This can be summed up as 'who is Deep Purple's true guitarist, Morse or Blackmore?'

It is odd that this debate has become — at times — so heated. No less a figure than Ken Hensley (keyboardist, sometime guitarist and overall creative lynchpin for the band Uriah Heep) wrote in his autobiography: 'When I see Steve Morse and Don Airey trying to be Ritchie Blackmore and Jon Lord- it doesn't work. They're great musicians, but with them, it isn't Deep Purple.'[4]

This, it must be said, is a harsh judgement. Deep Purple has always been a revolving door and most entrances and exits have not only passed off quietly but been widely appreciated for the injections of creativity that they have brought with them. When Gillan and Glover left in 1973 to be replaced by David Coverdale and Glenn Hughes, there was no real controversy, although the Mark III line-up has its own distinct devotees. Heck, even Blackmore's first departure — when Tommy Bolin gamely took over — has never caused much in the way of fan fights. Airey has been accepted with few complaints, but Morse often struggled to win fans over.

To some extent, this may reflect a nagging sense of underachievement around the band — certainly as they stood in the mid-2000s. As they took *Rapture Of The Deep* out on the road, the 'Morse era' had been going for twelve years, but had yet to produce anything truly exceptional.

On the one occasion when complacency had been confronted head on, *Bananas* had been the result — not a 'stand naked on top of it' effort by any stretch of the imagination. Fans could not entirely be blamed for wondering when, or if, this iteration of their favourite band was finally going to deliver.

Complicating matters was the fact that those fans were no longer concentrated in relatively small geographical and cultural spaces. World tours were by now genuine world tours and not slogs around the same well-worn paths over and over again. The 'new' fans that this more ambitious level of engagement had brought into the open had their own preferences and opinions. Deep Purple was now a truly global conversation with the Internet as the primary medium.

This was reflected in the songs that were included in set lists in different countries. The heady days of the *Purpendicular* tour were long over and more fixed patterns had begun to emerge.

On the whole, the less traditional destinations enjoyed more adventurous choices. For example, the set played at Cattolica in Italy on 10th July 2006 included no less than four songs from *Rapture Of The Deep*, as well as 'The Well Dressed Guitar' and a selection from across the older Mark II albums.

The balance of new material here was rarely matched in locations, such as the UK, where the band seemed to be wary of straying too far away from the tried and trusted. Nowhere was this better illustrated than by a UK tour in the early months of 2007 on which the intention was to play *Machine Head* in its entirety and in order.[5]

To some extent, this was simply to follow a then current fashion, with Deep Purple being anything but the only old rockers to subject their most prominent albums to such treatment.[6] In the event, it proved a bad move and the gimmick was dropped after a couple of dates, but it does underline a growing timidity around what might, or might not, be acceptable to core audiences.

It would be too simplistic to relate this back to the guitarist debate, but Morse seems to have been more readily accepted in the newer territories. Hensley proposes a reason for this, 'Steve's sound and technique is utterly different from Ritchie's. Maybe it is okay for people that only get to know Deep Purple now. For those who knew them in 1970/71 it isn't.[7]

An understandable comparison, this is still not very fair. The concerts from those distant days — as preserved on such recordings as *Stockholm 1970* — were essentially aural art installations. Two hours could be occupied by seven songs, at least two of which would be improvisations of half an hour each and longer.

Brilliant, yes, but not what a modern audience wants. Improvisation is still a requirement, but so is a larger number of songs and a sound that, in general, stays reasonably close to that of the studio takes. It all comes down to audience expectations. If Morse was not the Blackmore from days of yore, it was because he was giving his own audience what they wanted.

One of the more unusual audience requests came from the president of the Russian Federation. Dmitry Medvedev, a protégé of the outgoing Vladimir Putin, was elected on 2nd March 2008 and immediately appointed his predecessor to the post of Prime Minister. The media, unconvinced that this meant much had changed, dubbed the new arrangement a 'tandemocracy', in which the two men ruled as equals — more or less.

It is not the business of this book to comment on the politics of the former Soviet Union (although politics have entered the discussion more often than they would have done for a book about Deep Purple in the early seventies), but what is of relevance is Medvedev's musical tastes. He was a lifelong fan of heavy rock, his favourite bands being Black Sabbath, Led Zeppelin, Pink Floyd and, of course, Deep Purple. He supposedly had a large collection of vinyl records and had collected all of Deep Purple's works.

A sweet detail is that, as a youngster, he defied Communist-era proscriptions to make copies of his favourite albums, presumably on cassettes. In this respect, he was like many of his Western contemporaries. Perhaps one of the most regrettable consequences of the Internet's hegemony is its destruction and dismantling of the culture of creating home-made music collections on C90s. The 'mix tape' of favourites from different sources is a much-missed underground genre.

Medvedev was not unusual for a person from his background: a sizeable section of young Russians in the 1980s were devoted rockers, as Nicholas Blincoe has reported, 'My wife is a contemporary, attending Moscow State University at the same time Medvedev was at Leningrad State University. She recalls the student dorms echoing to rock, especially the holy triumvirate of Led Zeppelin, Deep Purple and Black Sabbath (though my wife continues to have a soft spot for Nazareth).'[8]

It was perhaps natural that Medvedev, on the cusp of becoming one of the world's most powerful people, would attempt to arrange a meeting with his rock idols. This first happened in February of 2008, just before the election that took him to power, when Deep Purple played at a concert in the Kremlin to celebrate the fifteenth anniversary of the Gazprom state natural gas monopoly (their contribution was — natch — 'Smoke On The Water').

Medvedev — considering who he was — came across as more than a little star struck: 'I was thirteen or fourteen when I first listened to Deep Purple, and such music was forbidden then,'[9] he said, adding, 'It would be completely surreal to imagine that I would meet this legendary band in the Kremlin, but it happened.'[10]

Gillan wrote an account of the event for the *Sunday Times*[11] in which he mentioned Medvedev's 'stupid grin' at meeting his favourite band, as well as noting some of the anxiety that still gripped people living in a country that had so recently been a totalitarian dictatorship: 'The Kremlin gig wasn't as straight as all that. The younger guys and more junior staff were all up on their feet, although they were looking nervously over at their bosses to see whether they could loosen their ties. It was as if they were asking, "How much fun are we allowed to have?"'

Films of the event certainly show the band having fun — and turning in a pretty decent performance of their most famous song to boot.

As bizarre as it might seem for a rock band from England to be in such a position, it was not the only time that it happened. In 2011, a more formal meeting was arranged. The band was on a short tour of Russia and was playing in Moscow on 23rd March, which presented the — by now — President with his opportunity.

The band were invited to tea at his luxurious villa just outside the city. Television news items and press pictures show Medvedev in semi-casual mode, wearing jeans and a dark jacket, a look shared by most members of the band. The meeting comes across as somewhat stilted — at least for as long as the small army of photographers hang around, crashing into things and generally getting in the way. Paice looks a little bemused, Morse shows some interest in the cold-war era reel-to-reel tape recorder from which some of the band's music plays as an ice-breaker. Glover is all politeness and propriety. When seated, with a cup of tea each, Gillan takes on the role of spokesman. According to *Reuters*, he joked that he had always thought that presidents were old men (Medvedev was 45 when the meeting took place).[12] Allegedly, with the press banished, Medvedev's son broke out a guitar for an impromptu jam with the band.

The episodes with Medvedev underline the way in which Deep Purple's position within the rock world was subtly changing. Put bluntly, they were getting older. Gillan had joked during interviews to publicise *Rapture Of The Deep* about what he had been doing on his sixtieth birthday. He makes for typically affable company — Gillan is a great talker and no mean raconteur — but sixty? Sixty? Were rock stars supposed to be that old?

To echo Gillan's words to Medvedev: we had always thought that rock stars were supposed to be young. The band had not been enfants terribles since well before the 1984 reformation, but neither had they been elder statesmen — except that, now, that's exactly what they were. Meeting presidents is perhaps what old rock stars are supposed to do.

In terms of the fans, it was another reason why matters were by no means as simple as they had been. Many — like Medvedev — were relatively advanced in age, having grown up with the band. At a gig in Birmingham in 2011, Gillan surveyed the rows of seated old timers in front of him and declared that he wanted them to stand up and get dancing. Given their average age, it was clear that they could do one or the other — doing both would have been a stretch.

But, then again, fans outside of the West were more likely to be of a different type: recent discoverers of the music, not lifelong devotees. Younger, then? The band certainly thought so.[13]

Perhaps that was why they were prepared to be more adventurous in those places. For the record, the set played in Moscow on the night of that second meeting with Medvedev featured songs from *Rapture Of The Deep*, *Bananas* and *Abandon*, as well as both of the instrumentals that had recently been recorded. The more established material included tracks from a range of albums, one new inclusion being 'Hard Lovin' Man' from *In Rock*.

Sounds like a gig worth being at…

9
One Eye To The Desert

The sales for *Rapture Of The Deep* were predictably low. Even worse than those for *Bananas*. Accumulated worldwide sales at the time of writing are an anaemic 220,000. In the light of such depressing statistics, some in the Purple camp were beginning to question whether recording new material was worth the effort.

This was certainly Morse's view: 'All indications for anybody who isn't doing rap music, why bother recording? Why bother making free downloads?'[1] He went on to clarify Deep Purple's position: 'The band really feels strongly that it's something that needs to be done to keep the band viable and renewed.'[2]

A major reason for the lack of new material was simply that Purple were — and always have been — an album band and the sad truth is that the album, as an art form, was on life support at best. This may sound over dramatic, but the decline in sales that Deep Purple experienced was far from unique. Everywhere and for everyone albums were no longer shifting in the volumes that they once had. This had much to do with the gradual loss of physical formats and, indeed, the very concept of owning music.

Of course, record shops still exist, but many are now, to all intents and purposes, peddling nostalgia — they hawk yesterday's technology to those who grew up with it and can't quite let go of it. This explains the resurgence of vinyl as a format in recent years. The claims that it sounds better than other formats are, frankly, nonsense. It sounds different, for sure, and that might be different in a way that suits a lot of people's tastes, but better? By what yardstick?

Most music, as Morse realised, is now online. It can be downloaded, or, more likely, streamed. For musicians, this presents a major problem — how to earn a living.[3] Fans no longer need to buy a whole album; they only need to download — and pay for — the tracks that they like. If they prefer to get their music from *Spotify*, or some such service, they will not own it at all and the royalty to the artist will be so minuscule that thousands of plays of a particular song will generate mere pennies in income.

The economist Alan Krueger[4] called this the 'Bowie Theory': ie: that recorded music has become so much a part of the very fabric of modern life that it has effectively been de-commodified and rendered devoid of any monetary value.

Pressure, then, is placed on the creation and curation of new material. There can be no filler, no 'end of side 2' tracks. Songs must be carefully placed next to each other in a way that encourages fans to buy the whole album and listen to it from start to finish. This goes for live albums, too, which, for Deep Purple at least, have proliferated in the twenty first century like never before.

Now, they tend to be recordings of full concerts, which has rarely been the case in the past. *Made In Japan* is a classic live album — perhaps *the* classic live album — but it does not preserve a full live performance. It is a collection of tracks that stand alone like the tracks on any other type of album.

There are silences between them, they do not represent all of the music played at a gig, they were not recorded at the same place, they were not recorded on the same night. *Made In Japan* is a live album, but it is not a concert album in the same way as, say, *Live At The Olympia*.

The message to potential buyers is clear: live albums are now about reliving the concert experience and that is hardly possible if all you have are tracks three, five and eight. You need to get the whole thing!

Morse was not alone in wondering what purpose recording new material might serve. It has been demonstrated that live performance is where the real money is to be earned and, as album sales have dropped off a cliff edge, so ticket prices have risen.[5]

This lies behind Deep Purple's diligence as far as gigging is concerned. Morse, even as early as 2004, spoke of how hard this could be: 'My wish is always that we'll do shorter tours in Deep Purple so that I can spend more time with my family, but if you are going to go on tour, it's a great band to do it with.'[6] Unfortunately for him, long tours are a necessity when they are your only means of paying the bills.

The upshot of all this was that the band entered a lengthy period in which no new recordings were forthcoming — or even seemed to be on the horizon. There were occasional murmurings about getting together to write something, usually in the form of an offhand comment in an interview, but no such activity occurred. Touring became, once again, the band's sole activity.

It would be fair to say, however, that the focus in touring was moving in response to changes in the habits of music consumers. Traditionally, a tour was undertaken to promote a new album. This was how the epic journey that had been Deep Purple's first, 1970s, incarnation had come to be.

Back then, the band put out records so often that they always had a 'latest release' to justify their presence on the road. As *Rapture Of The Deep* faded from the memory — and its songs began to be quietly dropped from the set list — this was increasingly no longer true. Touring became an end in itself. It was a chance to connect with fans, as well as keep the coffers topped up, but that was all; the days when gigs would debut early versions of songs that would soon be recorded in definitive form — as had been the case with 'Up The Wall'/ 'I Got Your Number' — were, for the moment, over.

The year 2007 began with a reminder that not all of the business around Blackmore's departure was yet over — neither would this be the last word. Sony BMG put out a recording of the 1993 NEC concert as part of a box set alongside one from Stuttgart made on the same tour.

Gillan almost immediately jumped in and blocked the release, his given reason being that he had not been informed about it. He told BBC Radio 4's *Today* programme that: 'It was one of the lowest points of my life — all of our lives.'[7]

His description of BMG executives as 'opportunistic fat cats' suggests his state of mind.[8] A BMG spokesman responded with: 'We are taking it off our sales platforms and trying to get back what there is out there. The CD has been out before in 1993, when it was sanctioned by the band.'[9]

The last part of this statement was correct. Not only had the video of *Come Hell Or High Water* been available for years (the CD with the same name and cover mostly featured songs from the Stuttgart gig), but Gillan had contributed a bespoke interview to it.

It is not certain, then, what motivated him to make a stand so long after the event. His claim that the performance had been 'awful' was not entirely fair. Yes, Blackmore had not been at his most inspired and enthusiastic, but his work was still professional and solid. The rest of the band did everything they could to compensate, being arguably better for doing so.

Gillan's attitude is perhaps an indication of how far the band had come in the fourteen years since that notorious night. When 'Come Hell…' was released, the Morse era was still in the future. A theme of the interviews on the video is a determination among the four remaining band members to continue and to not let the loss of their 'banjo player' be a fatal blow — although no one seemed to know quite how this was going to be accomplished.

For all anyone knew, those interviews could have been Deep Purple's last outputs as a living entity. Since then, it had become abundantly clear that the band were more than capable of surviving without Blackmore. Put simply, they had more power to dictate their own terms.

Other than that minor media fracas, this era of Deep Purple's history was spent in a typically arduous round of tours, including a long trip to the States and another series of dates in the UK, one being, ironically, at the NEC Arena. Halloween 2007 was spent in Romania, the home of Count Dracula.

With no new album on the way, or looking even remotely imminent, the focus shifted to individual projects, of which there were plenty on the go. It was Paice who, so to speak, set the pace, by engaging in a drum clinic in March 2007 (essentially a master class) at a place called Tom's Music Venue in Treforest, Wales. He also appeared at a gig in Italy in December with a band called Made. In ensuing years, he would emerge as one of the more active members outside the band, eventually finding himself playing with some unlikely collaborators.

Apart from Paice, it was the indefatigable Gillan who had a major moment with the release of his latest solo effort, *One Eye To Morocco*. Gillan explained the slightly odd title as coming from a conversation that he had in Kraków, Poland: 'I was in a café in the Jewish quarter there, talking to my friend about [Holocaust hero] Oskar Schindler, and a beautiful woman walked past and I lost concentration completely and followed her with my eyes and he said, "Ah, Ian, you have one eye to Morocco." Well, in English, we probably say "a wandering eye," but in Poland the expression is "one eye to Morocco and the other to the Caucasus," which literally means you're cross-eyed. You're looking in two directions at once.'[10]

The project came about when Deep Purple were temporarily pulled from the road in Spring 2008 as a result of

Roger Glover's mother dying, necessitating that he take a short break from band duties. Gillan went to Buffalo, New York, and set about using this unexpected free time productively.

His wingman was the ever-reliable Steve Morris. Thirty or so songs were written, or part-written, with the number whittled down as ideas were worked up into final products. A conscious decision was taken to make the album 'not a rock record', as Morris explained: 'Ian had an idea for the sound of the album he wanted and Nick Blagona the producer has helped him achieve this. It's a great sounding record, and in my opinion, helped by the fact there are no traditional solos as such, just guitar 'parts' and keyboard 'parts'. The songs and arrangements are the most important elements. In a way it's the complete antithesis to *Gillan's Inn*, where great solos hit you every few minutes. So it's a great and natural follow up record.'[11]

Gillan elaborated; 'I didn't want a heavy rhythm section with a lot of dramatic performance, I didn't want any guitar solos, improvised or otherwise — everything that's on there has been written, calculated to make the mood continuous. There's an intimacy about this that you won't get with a Deep Purple record.'[12]

All of that being said, the insistence that *One Eye To Morocco* is not a rock album cannot entirely be supported. Tracks such as, 'No Lotion For That' are not only unapologetic rock 'n' roll, but would not sound out of place on an old Gillan band album. 'Texas State Of Mind' — yes, it is here — is also a succulent slice of Southern Fried Boogie. For the most part, though, it is a blues and soul-infused collection — and an outstanding one at that. Without question an improvement on Deep Purple's most recent works, it again shows Gillan's growing willingness to stretch himself musically.

The title track, for instance, is one of his best ever songs, an evocative, moody, piece that — contrary to anecdotes about its origin — has a riff that is reminiscent of eastern music and some dreamily lilting cello among the guitars and saxophones. In places, it bears some similarities to late-period Beatles.

One Eye To Morocco is a fine addition to Gillan's oeuvre and further proof that Deep Purple was not a straitjacket for its members. Still, the main job beckoned and that meant getting back on tour. As the decade fizzled out, ever more inventive tactics were employed to coax punters to part with their cash for a ticket. Supporting acts that were draws in their own right were still proving successful, but so were more varied set lists.

Tours held during 2009 featured some of the boldest choices of material since *Purpendicular* and its associated gigs. At the NEC on 13th November, for example, the band played — along with the golden few that could never be dropped — 'Things I Never Said', 'Not Responsible' and 'Wasted Sunsets' (the last two coming from the 'Perfect Strangers' album), 'Rapture Of The Deep', 'Sometimes I Feel Like Screaming', 'Contact Lost', 'The Well Dressed Guitar', 'The Battle Rages On' and others that would generally be considered rarities. Most intriguingly, 'Wring That Neck' was wheeled out for a spin. There was no place for 'Perfect Strangers' and 'When A Blindman Cries'.

The emphasis on instrumentals and long solos suggests that, for whatever reason, Gillan's voice was being protected. Notwithstanding that, it is hard to escape the conclusion that an attempt was being made to 'freshen up' the live set. It is also noticeable that Morse era songs comprise a considerable portion of the running time.

On paper, it was all very exciting and worthy of celebration. After all, the *Machine Head*-from-start-to-finish idea had not worked out too well and it was good to hear songs that had mostly languished unloved on albums, finally blossoming in the live environment.

But the gigs were getting only a lukewarm reception from fans. It perhaps did not help that Gillan's stage banter was kept to a minimum: a vital connection to the audience was not being fully utilised. Reviews on sites such as *The Highway Star* were respectful rather than ecstatic. The virtuosity of the players was always recognised, but a lack of energy was all too often seen as the defining characteristic. The sense that the band were 'stuck in a rut' was becoming all pervasive. As a new decade dawned, it was glaringly obvious that some creative thinking was needed if the Deep Purple juggernaut was going to keep on rolling.

10
Strings Attached

Speaking to the *Birmingham Post* in 2009, Morse again expressed his view that recording was not top of his agenda: 'We're always trying to get started [on making a new album], but these tours keep popping up. Recording is very nearly a volunteer endeavour, and touring pays most of the bills. Despite that, as a group we are committed to doing a new record soon.'[1]

While such utterances left fans in little doubt that no fresh material was imminent, they were underscored by the reality that bringing some sense of novelty to the table was an urgent requirement. The band could hardly expect fans to keep turning up to the same gig over and over again. Structuring a gig around their biggest selling album had been tried, broadening the set list had been tried: it was time for a bolder move.

In March 2011 one was announced — a tour with an orchestra. Despite seeming to be a return to former glories, it would resolutely not be quite the same as orchestral collaborations of the past. Morse explained the intended approach: 'This one isn't going to be orchestra-based so much as, it's the rock band Deep Purple playing, with strings and horns being added for some colour textures. We're not going to change the songs — I mean, there will be a few little cameos and features — but the basic idea of the show is: we're doing what we do and having more texture where it's appropriate.'[2]

He went on to discuss some of the difficulties that pairing a rock band and an orchestra could cause — ones with which Sir Malcolm Arnold would have been familiar enough: 'Most important is keeping [classical musicians] on the beat with the music. A lot of classical players can read music great and everything, but the whole rhythm thing — maybe they don't feel how exact it needs to be to make rock 'n' roll rock.'³

Gillan, interviewed by Wolverhampton's *Express and Star*, added more detail: 'The orchestra is very much integrated into the band. We don't actually use them on every song. There are some songs where there's no validity for having an orchestra, which makes it even more dynamically interesting during the show. It's fantastic, when you hear something like 'Perfect Strangers', the orchestra gives such power to the riffs and to the structure of the song. And then you hear them swing like a train on songs like 'Lazy'. It's incredible, it's quite an experience. It's totally different to an ordinary Deep Purple show. It's edgy, very edgy… with lots of mistakes!'⁴

The conductor was to be Stephen Bentley-Klein. Fully loaded with the right classical credentials (studies at Guildhall School, London, and with Erik Friedman in New York), he nevertheless moved easily between worlds, being a master of classical, jazz, rock and ethnic music. His credits included stints with the National Theatre, working with such eminent directors as Trevor Nunn and Nicholas Hytner.

He had been concert master for the national treasure that is Shirley Bassey, as well as a Who's Who of other pop greats, ranging from Barry White to Rod Stewart to the Four Tops. He played on albums for the likes of Morcheeba, David Byrne and… the reader should by now have got the picture.

He was a serious player when it came to crossovers — genre being no object. His most direct connection to Deep Purple was through Airey, with whom he had played on Uli Roth's version of Vivaldi's *Four Seasons* — among other projects.

It was Airey who called and got him involved: 'He said Purple are going to go to America to do a tour and the promoters want them to do something different, you know. They hadn't been there for a few years and they wanted them to come back with something different and they were sort of thinking, they suggested an orchestra thing — are you interested?'[5]

The tour was billed as 'The Songs That Built Rock'. As a title, this is more than a little cheesy (it has a distinct whiff of James Last about it) and is quite a grandiose claim — Led Zeppelin and Black Sabbath fans, for example, might protest that their favourite bands did something to build rock, too — but it did foreground the idea that the tour would focus on the band's 'greatest hits'. There would be few entries in the set list from recent albums.

Bentley-Klein scored most of the orchestral parts, working, as he has said, mainly on his own: 'I didn't really talk to any of the band about how it was going to be, because they were like — we're just going to do our thing. I said, send me all the latest versions, the live versions of songs that you're playing at the show: there's no point going back to the records — I'll write the orchestra around what you're doing now.'[6]

From an early stage, he, in consultation with Bruce Payne, was determined to honour the notion that this was not to be, 'A classical Deep Purple, more like an expanded Deep Purple.'[7]

The setlist was, as might be expected, dominated by songs that leant themselves readily to interpretation by an orchestra — the Morse instrumentals, 'Rapture Of The Deep', 'Woman From Tokyo' (from the *Who Do We Think We Are* album), 'When A Blindman Cries', and so on. But there were also a couple that seemed left field, to say the least. 'Lazy', the *Machine Head* track referenced by Gillan, is essentially a blues jam in its basic form — it certainly does not, on the face of it, fit the kind of discipline required of an orchestra. If its inclusion is strange, stranger is the fact that it was used as a way to give Bentley-Klein a showcase violin solo.

Describing how this came about, he said: 'I was thinking from an early stage that it would be really good if we had a violin solo, which is, again — it surprises the audience. So we were in America and we were doing our shows. I wanted to get this solo in and I remember basically going, yeah, 'Lazy' would be good, I could jump in — and [the band] kept saying, let's get the New York shows out the way and then we'll throw it in. I said, no, we should get it in — I think it will really lift the show again. All shows need a point where they suddenly lift up again.'[8]

In this case, that lift came as the set was reaching its final third — the part that contained all the 'big hitters' from *Machine Head* and its ilk.

Even more unexpected than 'Lazy' is 'Hard Lovin' Man' from *In Rock*. This is arguably the heaviest song that the band have ever recorded, driven by a chugging riff, throbbing bass, uncompromising guitar solos and keyboards that sound like they are being played by someone in an advanced state of inebriation.

It is brilliant, but no song has less to offer people who play violins, trumpets and flutes — has it? Yet, it is not among the songs that serve to give the orchestra a breather: they are very much a part of it. Bentley-Klein's take was: 'When you get the set list, you look at the whole show and you have to go, what can I do there that will work really well? So you get a song like this and you go, what does this song need? What can I do that's a bit different to the other songs in order to bring out the special characteristics of the song?'[9]

Another contribution that the conductor made was to the start of the show. He told Bruce Payne that an opening in which nothing happened other than the orchestra tuning up, the conductor walking on and the band taking their positions would look drab and dull. Something more spectacular was required: 'We [the orchestra] need to play some kind of intro, so the band can come on to music and give them a slightly grander entrance, rather than coming on to Prokofiev, or something, played through the sound system. Bruce said, write something.'[10]

The result was a 1960s flavoured skiffle-based piece that resolved to a couple of riffs as a natural lead in to the show's first rock number, 'Highway Star'. The 'overture' had the additional benefit of bringing out the bluesy and jazzy qualities of the orchestral parts, underlining that this was not a primarily classical concert.

The tour began in Toronto with the band taking a typically improvisational approach; as Bentley-Klein remembers it: 'They said, we're going to have two or three days of rehearsals in Toronto and then we're off, up and running. So I said, okay, great. Then they said, you don't need to get to Toronto quite so early, something like a day later. Okay, so a day's rehearsal's gone missing. So I got there and the band were all there; we were having dinner and they said, actually we're not going to have any rehearsals — we're just going to have a rehearsal on the day.'[11] The final rehearsal was not, in the end, a whole day and did not involve everyone from the band.

Rehearsing was a problem throughout the North American leg. As with the 'Concerto' tour of a decade earlier, orchestras were mostly sourced from the areas visited, in order, as Morse put it, to help local music communities.[12]

Bentley-Klein also invited a few of his own contacts and friends to take part. Preparation time was at a premium. 'For a two-hour show, which had three or four instrumentals in it,' Bentley-Klein estimated, 'I had a two, two hour and a half, at most, rehearsal time and you'd have to stop and start all the time. I'm a great friend with Don and he just loves being involved with music and being around musicians, so he would say, "if we're in the same town in the afternoon… whenever I can, I will actually come down to you and just play the parts through with you."'[13]

Airey's willingness to given up his time had a number

of felicitous effects. He and Bentley-Klein worked out some moments — among the best in the final show — in which the keyboard solo section, which included extracts from classical pieces, was backed by the orchestra.

Paice began attending — largely because he realised how much fun it was to be in the rehearsals. With drums and keyboards helping the orchestra, the rehearsals became much more purposeful. In Europe similar problems were avoided because the New Frankfurt Philharmonia accompanied the band on all of their dates.

Bentley-Klein, still somewhat frazzled from the last-minute nature of it all, remembers feeling nervous on the first night in Toronto and being amazed when the band members all ordered themselves an alcoholic drink just before going on. Not wanting to seem like a 'square', he joined Airey in a brandy and had his eyes opened to what a good practice it was: the nerves drained away and he felt energised to head out on to the stage and give it his all.

In spite of Gillan's words about lots of mistakes, the shows were mostly slick and not afflicted by problems that the average audience member would notice. Bentley-Klein related one incident, which serves to illustrate how few major hiccups there actually were: 'Gillan used to do this joke where he had this little gong thing and he would stand up and just hit it and of course, there was a silence when he hit it, but Don would do a big gong sound. We decided that we would put that on the gong and on one of the shows we [Gillan and I] were chatting during the show… he was going, it's going really well B-K… we're really pleased with what you've done, it's great, it's fantastic. Then he went out and he did his gong thing and I had forgotten that Don was not going to do it and we were going to do it from the percussion section and I forgot to cue them and it went splash, you know. Then he came back to me and he went, mmm, maybe it's not going as well as I was saying.'[14]

Two documents from the tour are extant: CDs and DVDs of appearances at — obviously — the Montreux Jazz Festival on 16th July and the Verona Music Festival two nights later. Why two concerts were recorded is unclear, except that it can be presumed that they were intended to be each other's back up in the event of one or the other turning out to be unusable. Both being fine, it was judged that there was nothing to stop both being released. It should be said that the former was Deep Purple's latest entry in the long-running 'Live at Montreux' series.

Either can be chosen as evidence for the success of the tour. The Verona gig — which took place in the suitably monumental surroundings of the local Roman arena — begins with the brief jazzy orchestra-only Overture, which segues quite effectively into a crescendo from the band that kicks off a long, feedback-filled intro to 'Highway Star'.

The famous, epic, notes that begin the first verse bring the orchestra back. Every bit of promise is fulfilled. The brass and strings lend dimension and depth, so much so that the guitar and keyboard solos — when the orchestra drops to the background — sound thin by comparison.

The opener over, it is time for the insanity that is 'Hard Lovin' Man'. Listening to it is to suffer a form of musical cognitive dissonance, but in a good way. The orchestra match the band every step of the way. Airey's interpolating of classical quotations into his solo is a clever means of fusing the two halves. In every respect, it is stunning. Next comes another seldom-played song, 'Maybe I'm A Leo' from *Machine Head* (Airey going full Gershwin at one point), then 'Strange Kind Of Woman', then... It goes on, each song building on what has gone before, vindicating Bentley-Klein's words about looking at the whole show and how the different songs resonate with arch other. 'Rapture Of The Deep' becomes a mini-symphony, 'Lazy', duelling banjos as guitar and violin trade licks.

The one song that perhaps most benefits from the addition of an orchestra is 'Perfect Strangers'. Already an exercise in hugeness, the violins skittering over the main riff and the brass blasting its way into the silences between phrases take it to a whole new level.

As good as it is, Paul Mann maintains that the arrangement used was not one that had ever much appealed to Jon Lord. For all its grandeur, the song is basically a blues piece and quite dark, both in intention and execution: the 'show tune' version that became standard when it was played with an orchestra, to Lord, was inappropriate.

He may have had a point, but Mann's description of the orchestral elements as being reminiscent of incidental music from a seventies quiz show does seem a little extreme! As a whole, 'Perfect Strangers' with orchestra lives up to part of its title by being as close to perfection as crossover pieces get.

The concert as a whole is moving, surprising, jaw-dropping. Its venue would once have echoed to the clattering swords and pained screams of gladiators: it can be said with tongue only half in cheek that a not dissimilar level of intensity was achieved by the musicians who occupied the space on that night two millennia later.

Outside of the orchestra tour, the year was characteristically busy for Gillan, who was also engaged in a charity project with his old mate Tony Iommi. Going under the heading of *Who Cares*, it had its origins in the Rock Aid Armenia initiative from way back in 1988, when British musicians from a range of backgrounds had come together to raise money for victims of the Armenian earthquake of that year.

Broad in scope, it had produced several outputs, including a compilation album of such ill-thought out titles as 'Since You Been Gone' by Rainbow, 'All Right Now' by Free and 'We Built This City' by Starship. The only product that anyone really remembers, however, was a remake of 'Smoke On The Water' that featured a wet dream's worth of rock greats, including Iommi, Brian May, David Gilmour, Paul Rodgers, Keith Emerson… it would be tedious to list them all. From the Purple stable came Gillan and Blackmore.

The resulting single — on which the verses were sung by different vocalists — did well, entering the UK Top 40. A later rerelease, with an accompanying 'Making Of…' documentary on DVD brought in further funds.

The experience was the start of a lasting connection between Gillan and Armenia. *Who Cares* was thus very personal to him, its aim being the relatively modest one of enabling the building of a music school in the city of Gyumri; Gillan explained its genesis: 'I was called to Armenia to meet the president, and he said, "I remember this quotation, 'when you're ready for some music, we can do something'. So will you do something?" And it was perfect, they had this school that they didn't have funds for, and I think that music is a great symbol. It's very symbolic of people's culture.'[15]

Two songs were written and recorded, 'Out Of My Mind', and, 'Holy Water'. Both are tremendous chunks of rock on which Gillan and his collaborators are at their heavy best. And what collaborators they were! On the first song, Iommi supplied the guitar, but the two of them were ably backed up by a band that included Iron Maiden's Nicko McBrain on drums and one Jon Lord on keyboards.

'Holy Water' mixes its amped-up sounds with traditional Armenian instruments. The band is larger than for 'Out Of My Mind', with Gillan's usual partners in crime, Steve Morris and Michael Lee Jackson, playing lead roles.

The two new songs were later incorporated into another compilation album — one that was somewhat more essential than that which accompanied Rock Aid Armenia. It consisted of previously recorded tracks, as well as rarities and unreleased material from its, again, stellar line-up.

Although *Who Cares* generated nothing like the buzz of a Live Aid, a Live 8, or even a Rock Aid Armenia, it was a success, as Gillan pointed out: 'It's all going very well, I think they start building in a month or two. It's a fantastic story. We've got people in Canada sending musical instruments, we got a guy in England sending musical instruments. He shaved all his hair off and made fifty pounds to send to the fund. It's really fantastic.'[16]

The school was officially opened in September 2013. For his part in the endeavour, Gillan was awarded the honorary title of 'Friend of Armenians' by the Eastern Diocese of the Armenian Church in America. The ceremony took place in May 2014 in the Saint Vartan Cathedral in New York. Gillan spoke of how touched he was to be given the award: 'There was a time when people in Poland and German Democratic Republic were put into prison for listening to Deep Purple. I talked about it at my meeting with Dmitry Medvedev when he was the President of Russia. Now music helps us contribute to solving certain issues. This fantastic journey ended in September 2013 when we opened the school in Gyumri. But I believe new journeys are awaiting us.'[17]

It was a triumphant moment for Gillan, but *Who Cares* proved to have altogether greater significance for his erstwhile colleague, Jon Lord. The album was released on 13th July 2012, three days before a process that had commenced nearly a year earlier reached its inevitable culmination.

Even as Deep Purple were touring around the world with an orchestra, the man most closely associated with that style of music set out on his own journey, but it was not a fantastic one — it was not a fantastic one at all. A sudden, shocking announcement appeared on the Internet and in the press: Jon Lord was ill.

11
How Can I See When The Light Has Gone Out?

Lord had not wasted the decade since his departure from Deep Purple. He had realised his ambition to compose classical and classically-flavoured music — and then some.

His first outpouring, in 2004, had been *Beyond The Notes*, a collection of songs and tunes on which his chief collaborator had been Sam Brown, who wrote almost all of the lyrics.

He also composed a piano concerto entitled *Boom Of The Tingling Strings* and a lengthy piece in memory of the writer John Mortimer, *To Notice Such Things*, which is for solo flute, piano and string orchestra.

His masterpiece from this period, though, is undoubtedly *Durham Concerto*, a commission from the eponymous town's university as part of its 175th anniversary celebrations.

Lord himself concurred: 'I think it's probably the best thing I've done for orchestra because I think the orchestration itself is probably the best I've done. Whether musically I'd put it as the best... I'm certainly thrilled to bits with it.'[1] For the record, Paul Mann has stated that Lord was an outstanding orchestrator.

Lord was certainly cutting a very different figure from the one who had been Deep Purple's keyboard player for so many years. No longer the stick-thin hippyish type with long unkempt hair and a moustache that could hide a couple of Marshall amps, he had filled out and traded in the casual attire for a dark suit and waistcoat.

That hair, now pure white, was still worn long, but it was pulled back into the ponytail that became as much his trademark as twenty-minute Hammond Organ solos had once been. In other words, he had transitioned seamlessly from rock 'n' roll subculture to establishment high culture. Not, of course, that he had abandoned his roots completely.

He lent his talents to *Who Cares* and was also the main draw for a band calling itself The Hoochie Coochie Men, who produced two albums, one studio and one live. Best described as Lord's equivalent of Morse's *Living Loud*, he was typically enthusiastic about them: 'That was huge fun to do. I love playing that kind of blues, rock 'n' roll, r&b style. It's where I started with my first band; it was an r&b band.'[2]

He played the occasional gig in such a style, but his live performances were mostly now similar to those from the 'Concerto' tour. They consisted of a mixture of classical pieces and orchestra-backed rock. A few Deep Purple songs cropped up here and there, all given interesting new arrangements.

Yet, the *Concerto for Group and Orchestra* always exerted its pull. He could never quite get away from it — there was no particular reason to suppose that he wanted to. Performances of it took place all around the world. A notable instance was the Malcolm Arnold Festival in Northampton in 2007: Lord and Mann were there, as was Glover. The programme was a replica of that from the first performance in 1969. Despite all of this, no definitive studio recording had ever been made.

Lord started to put that right in the summer of 2011. But something else was occupying much of his head space. As he received an honorary doctorate from the university in the town of his birth, Leicester, he was conscious of a dull ache in his stomach: 'It was a kind of low-level discomfort, that's all. But just enough for you to notice it', he told Lee Marlow in *Classic Rock*.[3]

Two visits to the doctor convinced him that it was nothing

to worry about — even a specialist referral brought back a negative result. But, during one trip to the hospital, a chance cancellation meant that he was able to have an impromptu CAT scan, mainly in the spirit of ruling possibilities out. It was a life-changing moment. Summoned into a consultation room to be given the results, he heard the news that no one ever wants to hear; he had cancer. 'I realised, as I walked out of the hospital and down the street to my car,' he said, 'that something mighty had happened. That my life, as I knew it, would never be the same again. It was a heck of a blow.'[4]

He had pancreatic cancer, which Ian Paice described as 'not a good one.' It was not good in the sense that the prognosis was bleak: survival rates are very low. Nonetheless, Lord resolved to be positive, to beat it, to, above all, keep on working — in some form. The announcement on his website was vague, but it ruled out further touring — for the time being.

Expressions of support came in from all around the world, from the Deep Purple fan community, from the Jon Lord fan community and from the larger community of those who had known someone who had had the cancer, or who were fighting it themselves, or who were beating it. It was this last group that kept Lord going — they gave him hope.

He acknowledged the messages with an update that was more upbeat than the original announcement: 'Just a quick line or two from an absolutely overwhelmed, gratified and humbled musician. Your responses to the news of my condition have touched my heart in a way that has truly helped to make my life a better place to be than it had occasionally threatened to become these last few weeks.'[5]

The recording of the 'Concerto' was already underway when the diagnosis came. That project had its origins in a conversation over the kitchen table with Paul Mann, when someone — one of them — suggested that a definitive studio version was overdue. As Mann has said, there were, by that stage, some excellent live recordings available, but they were unavoidably prone to the potential liabilities of the concert context and did not necessarily represent the piece as Lord would ultimately want it to be.

Over the years, it had evolved, in part through Lord and Mann's tinkering, but also through interpretations by other performers, an example being the Australian band George, who radically rejigged it, much to Lord's delight.

The score was therefore gone back into so that things could be tightened, brightened and lightened. Marco De Goeij was invited back to look over the work.

It was important to Lord to let the piece speak for itself and to be seen as his composition and not as a Deep Purple product. In truth, it had always been that, properly regarded.

The recording of the 1969 concert was effectively a Lord solo album on which Deep Purple just happened to be playing; yes, Gillan (in collaboration with an allegedly half-pissed Malcolm Arnold) had supplied the lyrics, but every note of the music had been written and orchestrated by Lord, apart from the improvised 'group' solos.

New players could put their own spin on those, so Deep Purple were not, in the first instance, asked to take part. The idea began to form that the 'group' parts could be done on a 'horses for courses' basis — that the three movements could feature different soloists, the choices reflecting appropriateness to the music and not simple convenience.

From this came the suggestion that Lord could, 'Maybe divide up the singing,' as Mann put it, 'so that, you know, the first part of the singing could be done by a different person than the blues section.'[6]

The guitar soloist for the first movement was Darin Vasilev, a Hungarian who had already performed the 'Concerto' on stage, for the second, the blues powerhouse that is Joe Bonamassa.

Sourcing a player for the third movement proved to be more of a challenge. Lord and Mann were agreed that what they really wanted to reproduce was Steve Morse's performance from the 1999 revival — but who could possibly do that? A few names were mooted: a guy called Steve Morse got the job.

As for the vocals, the first part, the more folky and lyrical section, was turned into a two voice harmony for Steve Balsamo and the Polish singer Kasia Łaska. The later vocal verses — the rockier ones — were taken by the mighty Bruce Dickinson of Iron Maiden.

Both Paul Mann and Stephen Bentley-Klein have poured high praise upon Dickinson. Mann described him as having exactly the right sensibility for the 'Concerto' in his willingness to constantly look for new ways to add tone, texture and drama to his performance.

The recording got underway in Liverpool at the beginning of June 2011. Only the orchestra — the Liverpool Philharmonic — and the rhythm section were present. The plan was to add most of the group parts later.

For Mann, as conductor, the sessions threatened to be a tricky experience. The drummer, Brett Morgan, was in a different room, so could not be heard, only watched on a monitor and listened to through headphones.

Lord and Guy Pratt (the bass player) were to Mann's left, but were not amplified; Lord's Leslie speaker was, again, in a different room to allow for separation of the sounds and Pratt was playing into a recorder so that his contribution was audible only to himself. Fortunately, the Liverpool Philharmonic were already familiar with the piece, having performed it a year or so earlier.

As a consequence, the recording was, against the odds, relatively easy and trouble-free. Everything was completed in two days. Of the four sessions booked, only three were needed.

The tapes were then taken to Abbey Road Studios in

London for the laying down of the vocals and the group solo parts. Before this could happen, Lord received his diagnosis. His determination to keep working kept him focused, but, as Mann said, 'We tried to fit those sessions, the post-production sessions, around [Lord] as much as we could, to make sure that, you know, he was able to be involved as much as he still wanted to be. But, I think, in the end, it meant that I was much more involved in the production side than I would otherwise have been.'[7]

Understandably, Lord was absent for several key moments, such as the recording of Dickinson's vocals. Mann has spoken of the nervousness of all who had been in the studio about how Lord would react; if he did not like what he heard, the recording would have to be done again. Their concern was unwarranted: the genuine and spontaneous joy that Lord felt upon listening back to Dickinson's work is movingly preserved in a film of the sessions.

Of the recording as a whole, Mann has said, 'It represents a very strange combination of artistic enjoyment — and I had a wonderful time working with — and I'm still working with — Bruce Dickinson on this piece… and of course, the realisation that things were getting worse and worse for Jon.'[8]

The word from Lord's family was to be as positive as possible around him, but that the cancer was taking its toll is evident from the film, in which he appears physically reduced from the tall, commanding presence who had taken part in talks and Q&As only months earlier.

'He was very complicated in some respects, like all geniuses, I think,' Mann has said, 'He was not straightforward, but I think his essential nature was a positive one and although he sometimes needed help and encouragement to maintain that, I think that was his outlook. When [the diagnosis] happened, he will have known — like everyone knows — that pancreatic cancer is one of the most complicated cancers to treat and he would have known the situation that he was in, but we always tried around him to stay positive.'[9]

The final session took place in May 2012. It was to capture Vasilev's solo. Lord was able to listen to the finished recording; he said that he was happy with it: 'You can hear every note, every little nuance. Finally, we have that perfect balance between the instruments, which we didn't really capture — we didn't have the technology to capture — in 1969.'[10]

Listening to the recording at the remove of over a decade reveals the truth of what Lord was saying. Just as the 1999 revival does not sound exactly like the 1969 original, so the 2012 studio recording sounds like neither. To listen to all three alongside each other is to be reminded of how any piece of art created for performance is never fixed, but remains an organic, evolving entity.

The studio adds a layer of gloss not evident before, but the little tweaks and alterations shift the emphasis here and there, revealing emotional complexity in places, simplifying in others. The soloists own their work. Only Morse could be mistaken for Morse and none of them sound like Blackmore.

The vocals are lilting and beautiful in the hands of Balsamo and Łaska, visceral and passionate when Dickinson takes over. It is a fine recording of a masterpiece — there is no doubt about that — but the last word on it? If the history of the 'Concerto' has demonstrated anything, it is that there can never be a last word. Mann and Dickinson gave a number of concerts of the piece in Brazil in 2023: it had evolved once more.

While the 'Concerto' studio version was being brought to life, Lord was doing everything he could to cling on to life. Chemotherapy brought with it pain and the loss, after decades, of his ponytail. He undertook a trip to Israel to undergo an experimental procedure that called for him to be injected with bird flu.

This, allegedly, was a way to destroy cancerous cells. He

was lucky, he said, because, at his age, the cancer progressed slowly and had been caught early.

The tumour began to shrink. Light at the end of the tunnel! Perhaps, but all it revealed was the silhouette of a six-foot one inch man whose weight had dropped to under eleven stones and who had the thirty one inch waist he had last boasted as a poor musician in a small flat in the mid-sixties.

Inevitably, a plan was hatched to take the rejuvenated and — nearly — perfected 'Concerto' on the road. Lord was enthusiastic. Those plans never came to fruition. Jon Lord died of a pulmonary embolism on 16th July 2012. He did not live to see the studio version of the 'Concerto' hit the shops, meaning that *Who Cares* was the last of his recorded works to be released during his lifetime.

At least it was in a good cause. The *New York Times* was not alone in describing him as a heavy metal pioneer[11]: it is to be wondered whether he would have enjoyed the description. He was much, much more than that.

Paul Mann's last conversation with him had been a phone call from behind a pillar at Luton Airport around six weeks earlier: it was nothing important, nothing memorable, just a quick check in…

12
What Now?!

In the days that followed Lord's death, the media was filled with glowing tributes to him and his work. The jazz pianist Jamie Cullum, for example, called him a 'legend', former Guns N' Roses guitarist Slash wrote that Lord had produced, 'One of the biggest, baddest, heaviest sounds in heavy metal' and that he was 'one of a kind'. Even the actor Ewan McGregor wrote, 'Jon played with my great friend Tony Ashton. They'll be jamming upstairs now!'[1]

The members of Deep Purple — and former members — grieved in their own ways. Gillan described Lord as his 'hero', picking up on the word to recount a story about a starstruck fan in an airport who rushed up to Lord and, full of nerves, garbled, 'I'm your hero', to which the keyboardist insouciantly replied, 'So you're King Arthur.'

Morse recalled Lord's 'regal, gentlemanly manner', adding, 'Jon was the powerhouse keyboard player that brought rock and classical directly together many times.'

Glover found it 'unthinkable' that he was gone. Blackmore described Lord as not only a great musician, but his favourite dinner companion.[2]

He went on to provide one of the more moving memorials to his former colleague, an original instrumental called 'Carry On... Jon' that was added to the set lists of some Rainbow gigs in 2017. An acoustic piece filled with longing, it was basically a solo that was performed simply — Blackmore sat alone on an otherwise bare stage, picking at his guitar in honour of the man who had been his colleague, his rival, his source of frustration, but, perhaps, when all the nonsense was set aside, his friend. Nothing could more powerfully have demonstrated how much of a hole had been left in everyone's world by Lord's passing.

It was a huge loss to music, popular and classical. It also put paid to one of the odder ideas that was floating around at the time, a mooted reunion of Deep Purple Mark III.

Where this came from is uncertain, although it can be supposed that it emerged from the murk of fan chat that keeps the Internet in business. Glenn Hughes has maintained that most of the members of Mark III did have some conversations on the theme.

Presumably, it had occurred to someone that David Coverdale, as well as Hughes and Lord were not doing anything that they could not be persuaded to drop for as long it would take to produce an album and perhaps go on a tour.

Of course, Paice had been in Mark III and there was no sign of his wishing to quit the 'official' band to be a part of the project. Then there was Blackmore: without him, it would be a futile exercise.

Unfortunately, the plan was scuppered by his lack of availability — in the most straightforward sense of that term: 'We tried to privately get a reunion together,' Hughes said some years later, 'but we couldn't somehow, no one could get Ritchie on the phone. And after a while we just said, we gave it our best shot, and of course Jon was diagnosed and we had to let it go.'[3]

Hughes has claimed that even after Lord had gone, he, Coverdale and Blackmore talked about some sort of partial reunion. Coverdale has gone on record making cryptic references to this, too.

The closest it came to reality was the 2015 *Purple Album*, a collection of Mark III (and Mark IV) covers by Whitesnake.

To all intents and purposes, Coverdale's *Gillan's Inn*, it is an interesting addition to the Deep Purple universe, not least in how songs are rearranged and, in some cases, improved. Beyond that, it fails to tick the 'essential' box and has quickly been consigned to 'curio' status.

For Deep Purple, Lord's death was, for certain, a shattering blow, but life had to go on and that meant more touring. The lack of new material, however, was now becoming acute.

Gillan acknowledged as much at the Birmingham NEC stop on the 2011 orchestra tour, introducing 'Rapture Of The Deep' as the title track of the band's 'latest' album, saying rather sheepishly that it was 'about time' that they made a new one.

But no writing or recording was taking place or looked likely to be taking place any time soon. *Rapture Of The Deep* the album was increasingly being tacitly accepted by fans as the band's swansong — not the worst note on which to bow out, but nowhere near the best either.

It was at this point that Bob Ezrin started to take an interest. A Canadian by birth, Ezrin was primarily a music producer, but that is to be reductive to the point of absurdity. Michael Bradford was certainly no novice when he worked with Deep Purple, but even he would (probably) accept that he still had a long way to go before he could be ranked with Ezrin.

As a producer, Ezrin had worked with the likes of Alice Cooper, Aerosmith, Kiss and Andrea Bocelli. But his finest hour was arguably Pink Floyd's *The Wall*, which he co-produced with David Gilmour and Roger Waters.

A watershed double concept album made at the tail-end of the seventies, *The Wall* has resonated through the decades and has become universally accepted as one of the rock genre's greatest achievements.

For any band looking for creative input, Ezrin is as credentialed as they come, but he has a broad CV that takes in tech start-ups and, in an interesting piece of synchronicity with Gillan, the founding of a music-based school in Vancouver.

His philanthropy has included efforts to promote music

education in schools and, again recalling the work of members of Deep Purple, he recorded, in 2010, a charity single for victims of a massive earthquake in Haiti. Even as this chapter of the present book was being drafted, his contributions in a wide range of areas were recognised by his being named an Officer of the Order of Canada.

Ezrin's involvement with Deep Purple came about as a result of his being contacted by his friend Neil Warnock — Deep Purple's booking agent — who suggested that he produce the band's next album.

Ezrin was not the first in a similar position to have doubts. In his case, they were caused less by anything Deep Purple were doing than by his not wanting to be known only as a heavy rock producer. In a by-now familiar pattern, it was seeing the band live that changed his mind.

Attending a gig at Massey Hall in Toronto, he was — of course he was! — blown away by the virtuosity on display: 'They do this 'jam', which needs to be put in quotations because it is not just a jam, a lot of it is planned out. They do this 'jam' which lasts about ten or fifteen minutes where Morse steps up and is a total guitar god, and then Don backs him up with symphonic keyboards. The rhythm section comes in like rock gods, and suddenly, the whole hall is filled with this rock grandeur and this kind of energy that you never hear anymore.'[4]

Meeting with the band the next day, he posed a question that should probably have been put to them years earlier: what did they want to achieve with their next album? The consensus was overwhelming; they wanted to be Deep Purple. Not a radio-friendly band. Not a band producing songs of a standard length. Not a band producing songs in a single style.

Glover, in a seemingly throwaway, but ultimately influential, line said that he wanted to put the 'Deep' back into Purple. This meant writing with 'depth and meaning'. The nonsense songs of the *Abandon* era were not on the agenda.

Indeed, one of the defining characteristics of Deep Purple's work with Ezrin was not just a new lyrical seriousness, but a new sense of connection in the lyrics, a through line that builds through verses and choruses, rather than the old approach of verses being largely interchangeable (with 'Smoke On The Water' and a few others as notable exceptions).

'I remember you saying, stretch out,' Glover told Ezrin in a filmed conversation, 'and afterwards, after you'd gone, we said, what does that mean? Stretch out? Stretch out physically? Stretch out, longer songs? Stretch out every which way.'[5]

Part of Ezrin's avowed intent was to recreate something of what he had felt at Massey Hall: 'I think it was also important to capture the live sound of Deep Purple,' he has said. 'To me, that was essential. It was not only essential to capture that sound, but it was essential that they heard it when they came into the control room for the playback. I didn't want them coming into the control room and having an intellectual exercise reviewing the notes.'[6]

The band's 'homework' was to go away and think of how they could come up with 'musical pieces' rather than hard rock bashes. Such language, it need hardly be emphasised, borrows more from the lexicon of progressive, or 'prog', rock than heavy metal. Whatever would come of the collaboration with Ezrin, it was unlikely to too closely resemble *In Rock* or *Abandon*.

Everything came together in Nashville at a studio that Paice described as cavernous — a space to stretch out in, perhaps? Ezrin was a very different type of producer from Michael Bradford. Despite being a fine musician, his modus operandi was to let the band be the artists, intervening only occasionally to add grace notes and nips and tucks.

Still, he saw himself as the ultimate authority. Gillan spoke of him in surprisingly guarded terms: 'I thought he was a hard nut. He was quite disciplinarian. He was very professional. We have respect for him.'[7]

In interview after interview, the members of the band stated that what Ezrin brought to the party was 'focus.' His decisiveness was a key asset. Paice elucidated: 'Bob came out and told you in a very musical way where you had gone wrong, where you must go back to. And this could save you a couple of days of wasting time in the studio, when you have to go back to the beginning anyway. And he would say, "No, you were doing this. You changed it. It doesn't work. This is what you do to go back." So his musical impact was really important.'[8]

Gillan praised his attention to detail, remembering Ezrin giving him the somewhat pedantic direction: 'When you inhale, can you do it with more pathos?'[9]

Airey valued the way that Ezrin helped the musicians to resolve their music and ask what was the purpose of parts of the songs.

This ability to structure and identify the best outpourings from the band was a particular strength, because as they have always stressed, they do not write songs as such. That is why, in many ways, asking them to go away and think about what they were going to create was as far as they could go.

Instead, they jam, have fun, hit upon little riffs and runs which, only later, are hammered into the shape of a song. This makes Gillan's job especially difficult, in that he is given what amounts to an instrumental as a backing track and then has to superimpose a song on it; as Paice has said: 'We construct pieces of music. Once we are happy with the construction of this piece of music, we go to Ian [Gillan] and say, "Write a song on that!' I think only one time in thirty years we gave him something where he said, "Look, you have to change it. I can't write a song on this."'[10]

As haphazard as the process sounds, more often than not, it works, but the odd stinker here and there is a potent reminder of how easily it can go wrong. If Ezrin did anything, he took the broad view, surveying the band as a totality and pulling out what would work, while rejecting what would not.

The finished product went out under the title of *NOW What?!* This, apparently, was a humorous reference to the number of calls that the band were getting about making a new album: the exasperated tone of the phrase conveys how tired they were of having to answer the question.

The title also references time. Without anyone especially planning it, time became the big theme of this album and the two that followed it: fans took to referring to them as the 'Time Trilogy', even though the band never made any pronouncement to that effect. The albums were made by increasingly aged men — Gillan was nearly seventy and the others were not far behind. That they had mortality on their minds should surprise no one.

On which point, Jon Lord looms over the album like an invisible, but ever-present, spectre. Two songs are direct tributes to him. 'Above and Beyond' is particularly effective. Lyrically, it could be the words of Lord speaking to his old friends from the afterlife, from the — well — above and beyond. Gillan explained how they came about: 'Jon... filled the room and I wrote those words, 'souls had been touched, are forever entwined'. I sang them at his funeral and then I included them in the song, which was finished pretty much apart from that line. But when I wrote those words, it all made sense — and there was Jon Lord, singing to us.'[11]

Words aside, it is a strange song. Quiet, almost folky moments are contrasted with huge keyboard sounds that sound like orchestral brass. Something similar could be said for the other Lord tribute, 'Uncommon Man'. As its name implies, this bears some similarities to Copeland's 'Fanfare For The Common Man', especially in the rendition of it that was a hit for a band that Lord admired, Emerson Lake and Palmer.

Yet, it begins quietly, with Morse and Airey trading delicate wistful phrases. This goes on for nearly two minutes before Paice adds some abstract drum beats — not a groove, but texture. Only at around the two and a half minute mark does a consistent beat get going along with a riff which is overwhelmed by more huge, brassy keyboards.

By all accounts, the long 'prelude' was completely spontaneous, literally a jam. It is perhaps the best example on the album of the 'live feel' that Ezrin was hoping to evoke.

The 'Lord songs' are instructive in other ways. For a start, they are keyboard-led to an extent that was rare even during Lord's time with the band — and the sound is not that of a Hammond organ. It is that of a synthesiser. This was not unknown for Deep Purple; both of the Mark III albums, *Burn* and *Stormbringer*, had made extensive use of what had then been new technology. But, it was still a movement away from classic Deep Purple blues rock.

The opening track, 'A Simple Song', seems designed to accustom listeners to this. Not the uncompromising riff-driven ceiling-raiser that kicks off most Deep Purple albums, it begins with another Morse/Airey minimalist duet. Yes, it gets heavier later on, but this is no 'House Of Pain'. It is almost a song in chapters, with no single defining structure or melody. It is relatively complex for a simple song. It is also significant that the album's first sung word is 'time'.

The first single, 'All The Time In The World' continues to undermine expectations, with its country-style, laid back air. It is a good illustration of the band's working methods and one that demonstrates how tough it was to write the lyrics, as Gillan said: 'I had to do five rewrites on two of the songs on this album. Most of them were rewritten at least once or twice. 'Uncommon Man'… no, that was just a real problem song. 'All The Time In The World' and 'Weirdistan' — there were five completely different rewrites.'[12]

That notwithstanding, 'All The Time In The World' is one of Gillan's more amusing lyrics. Not the positive affirmation of other songs that share the same title, it is actually an idler's excuse for not doing anything. Particularly enjoyable are the lines:

'As everybody knows,
I may be slow, but I never quit.
Sometimes, on a good day, I sit and think,
Sometimes, I just sit'

The strangest song on the album is also one that was released as a single, 'Vincent Price'. Inspired by the eponymous actor, who had worked with Glover on the original *Butterfly Ball* project, it includes any number of features that were controversial on *Bananas*, but pass here without comment. Additional musicians? Mike Johnson plays steel guitar — in order to mimic the spooky tones of a theremin. Other voices? The introduction includes a choir; since no credit is given, it might be a sample, but, either way, it is not basic Deep Purple.

Structurally, it is also nothing like what had become a straitjacket on most recent albums, that pattern of intro - double verse - chorus - verse - chorus - solo - verse - chorus - outro.

It is not the only song to do this. Both Lord tribute songs, 'A Simple Song' and others play fast and loose with the formula. The single even had a video, which drolly alludes to the type of campy horror films for which Vincent Price is famous, although devotees of his work may not recall him ever running into a pole-dancing nun.

Taken as a whole, the album is a startling departure from what had come before. It is fresh and original and exciting. Gillan called it the band's best-sounding album and argued that it repositioned Deep Purple where they should be, as a primarily instrumental band. This is a self-effacing position that may be a coded acceptance of fading powers, but it also happens to be true.

It is remarkable how little singing there is. For minutes at a time, the only voices to be heard are those of Morse's guitar and Airey's keyboard. Especially Airey's keyboard, which is not insignificant, since it indicates a definite change of emphasis.

Whereas Deep Purple had always been a hard rock band that occasionally embraced prog, *NOW What?!* is unquestionably a prog album with occasional — very occasional — heavy parts.

It is worth asking why what was so badly misjudged on *Bananas* is so apt here. It may have been one of the aims of *NOW What?!* to bring the live experience into the studio, but that does not really come through strongly.

The album has levels of artifice to it that are unprecedented. It could perhaps be something as simple as timing. After such a long wait between studio albums, fans were happy to hear anything new. That it was so good was a bonus. They were certainly not going to complain about a few overdubs and sound effects.

It may also be that, in retrospect, Michael Bradford had laid the groundwork more successfully than had generally been appreciated: his interventions were controversial at the time, but, had he not made them, would Ezrin have been so readily accepted a decade later?

No discussion of the album's content would be complete without mentioning that it includes something that the band had eschewed since 1969, a cover version. They had rehashed one of their own songs on *Abandon*, but that did not really count. *NOW What?!* includes a full-blown reinterpretation of someone else's work.

The song in question is 'It'll Be Me', an old rock 'n' roll ditty by Jack Clement that had first been recorded by Jerry Lee Lewis in 1957. It is enjoyable enough — as much as it sounds like something from one of Gillan's solo live albums — and it is certainly done well, but it sticks out as an oddity. The band seemed to understand this, since it is listed as a 'bonus track', but it can be viewed as the beginning of a trend that would end badly some years later.

Carried on a wave of hype generated by a record company that knew how to do marketing properly, *NOW What?!* received some generally strong reviews — with a few reservations here and there.

Ultimate Classic Rock said of it: 'It's very good — or at least, the parts of it that are any good are very good.'[13]

Such sentiments were typical: after the critical drubbings that many of its predecessors had received, it was quietly contributing to the lifting of Deep Purple into that old rockers' stratosphere within which criticism ceases to be either honest or ironic to become, above all else, respectful.

This did not always equate to 'glowing' — *Ultimate Classic Rock* were, overall, only mildly enthusiastic about the album — but it did mean that the band were getting a fair hearing and that their prowess as musicians was being suitably acknowledged.

Pleasingly, *NOW What?!* did more than just appeal to journalists and commentators. It was a hit! A genuine chart-stormer! Sort of…

The ever-loyal Germans and Finns sent it to the top — or close to the top — of their countries' charts, and it sold well elsewhere, too. It claimed the number one spots in Austria and Norway and was only just outside the top 100 in the US.

In the UK, it was the first Deep Purple album in over two decades to make the Top 40, peaking at a very commendable 19. The 'but', though, is that it has, to date, still only shifted 300,000 copies worldwide — a bit more than *Bananas* and *Rapture Of The Deep*, but fewer than *Abandon* and everything that went before it.

This was the clearest indication so far of how patterns of consumption — and fandom — were changing. The album dealt with the subject of time and, if it was not, in and of itself, out of time exactly, it was being tossed on the sea of changing times, a product of a digital age of illusions (a Weirdistan, to use one of the album's song titles) in which something that would once have been condemned as another in a line of flops could be touted as a major success. And it was a success — the charts said so.

13
Sunflowers & Jam

In what had become standard practice, an expanded *NOW What?!* Gold Edition was released some months after the original. It added a few live takes on the songs, together with the usual oldies.

For some reason, instrumental-only cuts of several of the album's songs were included. The only new piece was the B-side 'First Sign Of Madness', which is not dissimilar to the 'Rapture'-era 'Things I Never Said', although not as good.

With Lord's passing still achingly close, disparate groups of people began to consider some sort of memorial to him. It might be said that the music did this already, but it was felt by many that something more definitive was needed.

Here was a man, after all, who commanded reverence from both the rock and classical communities. He was not just any old ivory-tickler. But there always seemed to be two separate Jon Lords — reconciling the skinny hippy with the white-haired establishment figure took a big mental leap. Whatever was decided upon would have to do something to bring the two together.

In the end, the vehicle was the *Sunflower Jam*. This was essentially a charitable organisation, set up by Jacky Paice, wife of Ian, that put on charitable concerts ('Sunflower Jams') in order to raise money for alternative carers for cancer victims.

Given its pedigree, it was able to regularly attract some of the biggest names in rock. Lord had been a big supporter, appearing on almost every occasion. The first few had been held at Porchester Hall in London, a relatively modest venue that ensured exclusivity. With high ticket prices and limited guest lists, the Jams were not strictly speaking 'public' events.

The scale increased in 2011 with the 'Superjam', which was held at the Royal Albert Hall. Anyone who wished to, and could afford it, could go along to that one. Deep Purple broke off from the orchestra tour to appear, taking Stephen Bentley-Klein (but no orchestra) with them. He has said of it: '[Lord] was rehearsing for the show and Rick Wakeman was there and they were going to do [the David Bowie song] 'Life On Mars' and they said, "Oh, yeah, we're doing 'Life On Mars' — we need some violin on that," so I got roped into that — you know how you do.'[1]

Bentley-Klein has said that, during this encounter, Lord expressed doubts to him about the wisdom of Deep Purple going out on tour with an orchestra — an indication, perhaps, of the complexity of character to which Paul Mann has alluded.

That night in 2011 was seen by many — not least Lord himself, as something of a crowning glory for his career. It was also the last time that Lord and Deep Purple shared a stage — although they performed separate sets. It was therefore natural that a deluxe repeat — a supersuperjam? — should be the means of giving the maestro a proper send-off.

The charitable aspect having a focus on cancer sufferers made it doubly appropriate. Paul Mann has suggested that it came out of discussions following Lord's funeral, for which he had arranged the music. He and Lord's wife liked the idea of a concert, but they were united in not wanting it to have the feel of a requiem or memorial; something more upbeat, more celebratory, was their favoured direction.

Ian Paice described the initial impetus for what eventually emerged: 'We wanted to incorporate a little bit of each incarnation of Jon's successful musical life, from [pre-Purple sixties band] The Artwoods onwards. We wanted everybody on stage to be connected with Jon, either musically or personally. We needed to have that sort of camaraderie on stage.'[2]

The orchestral contributions were to be conducted by Paul Mann, who was brought in because, as he said: 'By that stage, I must have been regarded by Jon's family as his musical right-hand man — I don't know how they would put it — I wouldn't want to put words in their mouths. Certainly, they recognised the nature of the relationship that Jon and I had'[3] — that of both friend and collaborator.

The classical parts were to be played by the Orion Orchestra, who, in the spirit of the event, are themselves a social enterprise that aims to give performance opportunities to young and aspiring musicians.

As the list of performers came together, some names were predictable, others less so. In the former camp were Deep Purple — obviously — Glenn Hughes — also obviously — Bruce Dickinson — less obviously than might be supposed — Steve Balsamo and Miller Anderson.

The latter group included such unexpected members as Sandy Thom, Jeremy Irons and Paul Weller, the last of whom had had little to do with Lord and was not known for either rock or classical music.

Ian Paice explained his inclusion: 'That came from the first *Sunflower Jam* in 2006, when Paul and Robert Plant both kindly offered to help. At the end of the night there was a big jam and Paul found himself on stage with Jon and me. So, when we lost Jon and Jacky was putting this together, Paul was one of the first guys to say: "I'll be there."'[4]

Weller ended up playing The Artwoods songs, 'Things Get Better' and 'I Take What I Want', Paice arguing that he had the right voice and attitude for those pieces.

There were some glaring omissions. Coverdale was nowhere to be seen, the given reason being that he was tied up in the studio and could not spare what would have been a minimum of several days to attend.

A bizarre absence was that of bassist Nick Simper, with whom Lord had played in The Flowerpot Men and Mark I Deep Purple. The biggest hole in the dramatis personae, however, was undoubtedly Ritchie Blackmore. According to Paice, 'He chose to do his own contribution in his own way. He wrote a lovely piece of music and dedicated it to Jon. That's what he wanted to do and that's fine. He's a man who drives his own course through life anyway.'[5] The piece was, as mentioned in a previous chapter, 'Carry On…Jon'.

Curating the programme took some time — as Mann has said, any celebration of Lord's life could have gone on for twelve hours or more. The whittling down process was not easy and it did not preclude the evening from being a long one.

A key question was how everything would be structured. Mann has said that his initial idea was for the first half to represent Lord as a composer, with the rest showing his trajectory as a rock musician. Paice spoke of a chronological arrangement — which would have seen rock and classical pieces alternating — being briefly considered, but quickly dropped in the face of the technical difficulties that it would present. The final programme took the form described by Mann.

Like the 'Concerto' shows that had taken place in the same location fifteen years earlier, it was an enormous operation. The number of participants was huge. None were being paid, but many had to be brought in from around the world.

The line-up was incredibly starry — so much so that Neil Murray, who is not what would conventionally be described as 'obscure' in his own right — was relegated to the 'house band' that boosted some of the rock songs and provided any electrical parts needed during the classical section. But everything came together very smoothly and quickly, powered by the goodwill that Lord had generated over the decades.

It was an excited and expectant audience that assembled in the Royal Albert Hall on a pleasant April evening in 2014. Master of Ceremonies was 'Whispering' Bob Harris, who was best known as the host of the long-defunct TV music show, *The Old Grey Whistle Test*.

The concert began with some selections from *Sarabande*, the first of several extracts from that composition that were scattered around the first half. In one instance they allowed for a guest slot from Rick Wakeman. The opening movement of *Durham Concerto* was also given an airing.

Interspersed with these were some of the pieces that showcased Lord's ability to mix classical and popular music. Premiering was a song called 'All Those Years Ago' that featured Steve Balsamo, the violinist Anna Phoebe, with whom Lord had worked, and his old Whitesnake sparring partner Mickey Moody.

'Pictured Within' with Miller Anderson was included as was 'One From The Meadow' with Margo Buchanan standing in for Sam Brown, who, by that stage, was undergoing her own struggles, having lost her singing voice some years earlier.

Mann has accepted that not everyone thought that this was a good inclusion, but that it was 'very Jon' and that it was one of which he had been particularly fond. He had been wont to go out walking with his dogs and the song was a genuine expression of his love for the English countryside.

The first half ended on a high, despite being probably the least showy part of the evening, when Jeremy Irons reprised his performance from *To Notice Such Things* reading Thomas Hardy's poem 'Afterwards' over a simple piano backing: 'The thing that I'm proudest of that night actually was that little moment,' Mann has said, 'After all the stuff with the orchestra and all the jumping around, for me to have to sit there and focus on the piano and play that very subtle thing was probably the biggest challenge at that concert.'[6]

Strangely, the classical half included nothing from *Concerto for Group and Orchestra*. The reasons were both artistic and practical. According to Paice, it was all about giving space to some of Lord's lesser-known compositions, the 'Concerto' already having a considerable presence in the marketplace — most recently via the studio recording.

Mann suggested that it would have been difficult to choose an extract that would have properly represented the piece: playing an entire movement would have meant committing nearly twenty minutes of the evening to a single work, which, to agree with Paice, was already quite well known. Moving into the second half of the evening, this was not to be the only time that fans found themselves checking their programmes in anticipation of something that proved not to be there.

After the interval, Weller performed his two songs, the first suffering a false start that had him reassuring the audience that he had actually rehearsed them. Then a scratch band that included Paice and former Whitesnake guitarist Bernie Marsden did a couple of numbers from the catalogue of Paice, Ashton and Lord, a short-lived project that filled the gap between Deep Purple's split in 1976 and the recruitment of two of its members into Whitesnake.

Next up was a lovely mainly-orchestra version of Mark III's 'Soldier of Fortune' sung by Steve Balsamo and Sandy Thom. Supposedly one of Lord's favourite Deep Purple songs, which often appeared on the set list of his solo concerts, it is a strange choice since Blackmore and Coverdale are its only credited writers.

Glenn Hughes and Bruce Dickinson (with a backing band that included Paice and Airey) followed up with duet versions of 'Burn' and 'You Keep On Moving' (from *Come Taste the Band*). Before Hughes took the stage alone to sing his Stevie Wonderesque 'This Time Around', a song that only he appears to believe is a classic — although his performance was superb.

From there on, it was Deep Purple all the way. Dickinson gave them an introduction in which he intended to build up to the revelation that they were about to appear, but he fluffed his lines and let the cat out of the bag earlier than intended. It was not much of a secret, to be fair.

The band's set was intriguing in a number of ways. It began, as might be expected, with the two Lord tribute songs from *NOW What?!*, before moving on to 'Lazy', with a cameo from Stephen Bentley-Klein. The version of 'Perfect Strangers' began with an orchestral lead-in that Lord had composed, but which had not hitherto ever been performed. Mann described it as a 'Liszt Hungarian rhapsody' inspired by the augmented second that ran throughout the song.

'It's difficult to play,' he went on, 'and tricky to conduct and really effective. The way that [Lord] makes the organ entrance that starts 'Perfect Strangers' sneak in quietly underneath the orchestra and then there's kind of a shriek in the orchestra and a big kind of crescendo and then the band thing starts — it's one of the most effective things.'[7]

The set ended with a long jam-heavy version of 'Hush' with which everyone — all the singers, all the musicians, the orchestra — got involved.

Its centrepiece was a keyboard duel between Airey and Wakeman in which, comically, the latter failed, at first, to spot a riff from one of the songs that he had written for the band Yes.

Given how much 'Hush' is driven by keyboards, it was a very fitting way to bring proceedings to a close. There was no 'Smoke On The Water', which must have made it the only Deep Purple gig in forty or so years in which that old warhorse was given a night off. But that, too, was fitting. 'Smoke' has always been about Gillan's lyrics and — pre-eminently — Blackmore's riff. It is not a 'Jon Lord song' as such.

The same could be said of songs from the Whitesnake cannon, which were also nowhere to be heard, in spite of the presence of several former members of that band, not least Airey and Paice.

Paice stated that the reason was that artists were allowed to choose their own material and no one opted for anything by Whitesnake. It must be admitted that the evening would have been one of extremes had it contained both a British acting icon intoning the words of Thomas Hardy and someone singing, 'I wanna slide it in right to the top'.

At the end, the crowd hung around for an encore (irrespective of the evening having already lasted for ages), but Dickinson put paid to that when he jokily told everyone to 'go home'. The audience cannot be entirely blamed. It was a wonderful occasion — and the music was not all that there was to it.

Lord's widow read a moving statement and Joe Brown, father of Sam and sixties hitmaker, turned up to pay tribute, stressing how much of a friend Lord had been to his family. Gillan re-told the story of how he had come up with the lyrics to *Concerto for Group and Orchestra*, producing the famous napkin on which he had written them down at the last minute. It may have been the actual napkin. It was certainly a napkin.

How much the concert raised for its good causes is not easy to ascertain, but a substantial amount can be supposed. The two halves were later given separate album releases. Records of an evening of celebration and love.

Back in the real world, everyone was about to get a reminder of the discord that had always been part of the Deep Purple story. Sunflowers aside, a former member had come to the conclusion that he was not getting as much jam as he should have been.

The *Guardian* reported that Blackmore had begun a legal action to reclaim some £750,000 in unpaid royalties, as well as enhanced royalties from all the Deep Purple albums on which he had appeared (and for which he had been the main writer).[8]

This followed a similar action by the other members of the Mark II line up, the defendants being the management companies Deep Purple (Overseas) Ltd and HEC Enterprises.

Blackmore found himself falling down something of a rabbit hole. As investigations into Deep Purple's financials were carried out, it began to appear that there was more to the case than anyone had initially thought. Money had gone missing from both companies and everything pointed to the band's accountant, Dipak Rao, being culpable.[9]

Over a period of seven years, he was found to have been coolly helping himself to funds totalling some £2.4 million. But, as criminal masterminds go, he seems to have been closer to Dr Evil than Professor Moriarty. His efforts to cover his tracks included, for instance, making the bizarre claim that 'boiler room' fraudsters were responsible for the theft.[10]

The consequences of his actions were severe for both himself and the two management companies. He was sentenced to six years and four months in prison for fraud and money laundering, they were wound up. A new company, Purpletuity, was set up, of which Gillan and Paice, as well as Blackmore's manager Carole Stevens were among the directors.

To mark their victory, the Surrey police who had investigated the case made a pop video on the steps of Guildford Crown Court with local singer-songwriter Leoni Jane Kennedy.[11] It has not been posted to YouTube.

Whether Blackmore got his money is a different matter. Shortly after he launched his action, he announced a money-spinning part reformation of Rainbow. There may be no connection between the two things.

14
Inducted

An entirely self-appointed body, the Rock and Roll Hall of Fame has, even so, become accepted as the arbiter of what is worthy — which is not necessarily the same as 'good' — in popular music. Admission to the hallowed inner circle that it represents is to be accepted into a form of cultural aristocracy.

Founded in 1983 by Ahmet Ertegun, chairman of Capitol Records, and located in Cleveland, Ohio, the Hall is essentially a museum, although that is a bit like saying that Michelin is essentially a tyre company.

Both statements are true, but they only go so far. According to the Hall of Fame's website, 'One of the Foundation's many functions is to recognise the contributions of those who have had a significant impact on the evolution, development and perpetuation of rock and roll'.

This is done by 'inducting' a number of acts every year. That number is small and inclusion within it comes as a result of being nominated and chosen by a committee. This process results in many being called, but few chosen.

The criteria for selection are as arcane as those for most such awards. The only fixed requirement is that a nominee needs to have released their first recording no later than twenty-five years previously. Beyond that, those who run the Hall freely admit that it all comes down to interpretation. Number of records sold, number of top ten hits attained, number of countries gigged in — all are irrelevant, or, at least, no more than persuasive. Statistics are not the deciding factor.

The induction takes place at a lavish annual ceremony held somewhere in the United States, at which one of an inductee's peers makes a speech of introduction before presenting the award. The newly minted members of the Hall then make a few speeches of their own, before performing three of their songs.

This is to state baldly what has become the occasion for some historic, and often unlikely, reunions. Former musical colleagues who have barely spoken to each other for years have been talked into sharing a stage at the ceremony, perhaps for the last time. One of the more notable examples was that of The Four Seasons, who briefly reformed for their 1990 induction, an event so significant that it provided the finale for 'Jersey Boys', a jukebox musical based on their career.

Deep Purple — as the above more than confirms — were ripe for induction. Indeed, by the mid-2010s, the Morse iteration was not far from meeting the basic requirement in its own right. Deep Purple the brand were so venerable that their reformation – reformation! - was very nearly contemporaneous with the founding of the Hall — to not even mention everything that had gone before. As for importance and influence: well, how long have you got? To sum it up in four words, 'Smoke On The Water'.

Yet, Deep Purple were not in the Hall, although it was not for lack of conversation about the subject. Interviews increasingly brought it up. Speaking in 2013, Gillan gave his usual answer, trying to sound insouciant, but coming across as a little disingenuous: 'I'm not too concerned about it. Maybe it will happen one day, but if not, my diary is full and I'm very happy. It hasn't affected our career but it does concern the fans — that's who I feel for.'[1]

He was right there. Fans were the driving force, demonstrating again how powerful they had become in the

Internet and social media age. A Facebook page devoted to campaigning on the band's behalf existed. In fact, there was at least one page. The clamour was getting ever louder. Plenty of Deep Purple's peers added their voices, lobbying for their inclusion. These included Geddy Lee of Rush, Kiss's Gene Simmons and, perhaps above all, Metallica's drummer Lars Ulrich.

They all had a point. The other two behemoths of seventies hard rock — Led Zeppelin and Black Sabbath — had long since been inducted. Moreover, the full list of past inductees included a few odd names, bands and individuals who could not, in all honesty, be said to have made that significant a contribution to the development of popular music. The Dells, anyone? A great act, no doubt, but did one of their members write a Concerto?

There had been some near misses. First eligible in 1994, Deep Purple were nominated in 2013 and 2014, to no avail. It is difficult to understand why the committee decided to pass on them, but Glover suggested that a truly incomprehensible reason was given: 'One of the jurors was heard to say, "You know, Deep Purple: they're just one hit wonders." How can you deal with that kind of philistinism?'[2]

Following on from that, speaking to Chile's *Radio Futuro*, Gillan said: 'Whatever I say about that is gonna sound wrong. But who the hell wants to be in an institution? The Hall Of Fame thing, it's an American thing. We don't have that in England or Germany or Australia or Russia or anywhere in the world apart from America. And it's an institution. What's that got to do with rock and roll? Also, it's run by these old guys who thought that The Monkees were America's answer to The Beatles. And they called Deep Purple [Laughs]… I don't think they quite understand what we are… They called us one-hit wonders. So I don't know what they were talking about… whether it was 'Hush' or 'Black Night' or 'Strange Kind Of Woman', 'Smoke On The Water', 'Child In Time', 'Knocking

At Your Back Door' or one of those one-hit wonders that we were... 'Highway Star'... I just don't know. And I guess the fans don't really understand it except in America. It's no big deal.'

While the view to which Glover and Gillan were alluding was not exactly understandable, it did touch on one inescapable fact: the band's almost total lack of visibility in the USA, House of Blues tours and their ilk notwithstanding.

To be sure, this was a relatively recent thing. In 1974, they had been the biggest game in town, to the extent that they headlined the so-called 'California Jam' festival. As gigs go, it was only marginally less controversial than the NEC in '93. But, still, it did not prevent most people in Cleveland, Ohio, really having no clue who they were. Glover went on to state the official line that the band were not bothered, that it should have happened when Lord was still alive, that it would only be for the fans anyway and that...

In 2016, it happened. It was announced that Deep Purple were to be inducted. Sort of...

The citation only mentioned Marks I to III — and not even all the members of those. Blackmore, Paice and — posthumously — Lord were safe, as were Gillan and Glover. Coverdale and Hughes also received invites and so did Rod Evans, the Mark I lead singer. But there was no mention of Nick Simper. His attitude echoed that of many fans: 'Maybe I am being naïve, but I always thought that if a band gets into the Hall of Fame, then all members, past and present, are part of it. Obviously not. Yes, it's a little strange that I am the only one from Marks I, II and III being left out, but I shan't lose any sleep over this.'[3] Quite why it happened is a mystery. No reason has ever been given.

Potentially more serious was the fact that there was to be no induction for all of the current members. Morse had given twenty-two years off his life to the band; Airey, the 'new kid on the block', had been around for fourteen. Both were ruthlessly ignored. But that was not the main problem. Not by a long way. Regarding Evans: he had not been heard from since 1980. Literally, he had not been heard from. No one knew where he was or what he was doing. People in witness protection have more public presence.[4]

Then there was the man in black himself: Ritchie Blackmore. Who knew what would happen if he turned up? Paice, talking to *Rolling Stone* magazine, summed up what was on everyone's mind: 'We have to accept that there are personalities that don't see eye-to-eye in our history. How [Blackmore attending] would work, I have no idea. Whether that could be put aside, I don't know.'[4]

Gillan cleared things up from his perspective: 'It would be unconscionable to think about bringing Ritchie in. I don't have an issue with Ritchie, nor does anyone. I've been in touch with Ritchie recently and everything's cool, so there's no bitter personal problem. We're too old for that and everything's in the past, but no. That would be out of the question.'[5]

The question resolved itself into that of who would perform the band's three songs. If Blackmore were there, would he bump the non-inductee Morse? Would Coverdale and Hughes sing along with Gillan? The opportunity for two thirds of this to happen at the Celebrating Jon Lord concert had not been taken. What about the keyboard parts? The only one who could possibly play those was Airey, but why include him and not Morse? It was, of course, lost on no one (other than, perhaps, the band themselves) that something like Lord's dream-that-was-never-actually-a-dream could, in part, come true.

Gillan took a hard line, threatening to boycott the event if Morse and Airey could not be a part of it. Posting on his website, he likened it to being invited to a wedding to which his family were not also invited and at which he would be obliged to sit next to his long-out-of-the-picture ex. The post ended with a clear statement that he would be declining the invitation.

The Blackmore dilemma was apparently resolved when the guitarist announced that he would not be attending. Joel Peresman, the Hall's president, gave for this the apparently innocuous reason that Blackmore was due to have surgery on his hand at around the time of the ceremony and so could not make it. Perhaps that was the case, perhaps it was not, because it has never really been ascertained why Blackmore made his decision.

At the time, perhaps mischievously, given his loathing of such events, he claimed that he wanted to go, but had been prevented from doing so by Bruce Payne. Coverdale gave his backing to this version some years later: 'I was only concerned about Glenn Hughes. The rest of 'em I haven't got time for. They prevented Ritchie Blackmore from coming in to be honoured as a Rock and Roll Hall of Famer.'[7]

He subsequently doubled down on this, saying that the band's management had tried to stop him and Hughes from even making speeches, let alone performing. He added the fair point that none of them would have been inducted at all had it not been for Blackmore.[8]

For their part, the continuity band have denied that they excluded Blackmore. Speaking in 2021, Gillan said: 'I hear David Coverdale and others talking about what happened at the Rock And Roll Hall Of Fame. Well, we were very kind to everybody, the current band. And we did invite Ritchie to play 'Smoke On The Water' with us at the ceremony, but he declined. So, [those] are just opportunistic remarks from the others.'[9]

Whichever version is true, it can be stated with certainty that a compromise was reached which would involve all inductees who bothered to turn up making speeches, but only the current band performing. Quite how Morse and Airey — gatecrashers at their own party — felt about this has not been recorded.

There had thus been enough drama for a Netflix special

before anyone even assembled at Brooklyn's Barclays Center on the evening of 11th April for the actual ceremony. Lacking a single compere, it was focused on the acts and those who introduced them. In Deep Purple's case, this was Lars Ulrich.

That he was a fan was obvious. He spoke about the band's history and said nice things about the individual members who were being inducted. To Rod Evans, he sent out a plea to not 'be shy' and come forward (Evans is yet to do so). Predictably, the biggest cheer came when he brought up the name of 'Ritchie fuckin' Blackmore.'

The band's speeches were mostly standard issue 'thanks to everyone' orations. Gillan added a few barbs on behalf of Morse and Airey. Coverdale spent a large chunk of his allotted time harping on about Whitesnake: it was perhaps a tacit admission that their day of standing there would never come.

That all done, the audience was treated to versions of 'Highway Star', 'Smoke On The Water' and 'Hush'. The last of these, of course, was not the band's song, but, then again, neither was the instrumental lead-in to it, a version of Booker T and the MGs' 'Green Onions'.

As sets go, it was played with characteristic panache and the brief jam with which the band ended 'Smoke' was a definite crowd pleaser. Nonetheless, it was hard for the fans who had longed for that moment not to feel cheated. The current band could be seen any time - any time that they toured, at least. But 'Smoke On The Water' with Blackmore (and why not Morse) and verses sung by Gillan, Hughes and Coverdale: that would have been life-changing.

It was not to be. Everyone packed up and went their separate ways again. There was plenty to be getting on with.

For Gillan, that meant another solo tour. It was to be another outing for band and orchestra, this time for a select number of dates in Eastern Europe. The set list would consist of a mixture of Gillan's own songs interspersed with items from the Deep Purple catalogue. It was not to be a repeat of the *Gillan's Inn* tour: this time, Deep Purple's music was to very much take pride of place. Indeed, in terms of structure, the set list resembled nothing so much as that of Blackmore's revived Rainbow gigs.

The solo songs were pretty much what might be expected: 'Hang Me Out To Dry', 'A Day Late And A Dollar Short' and a hugely ambitious rendition of 'No More Cane On The Brazos.'

More interesting was the choice of Deep Purple songs. Gillan quite deliberately and self-consciously took the opportunity to perform some of his favourites, the ones that had been either partly, or totally, ignored in the live setting up to that point. So 'Anya', from *The Battle Rages On…* was brought back after many years in the wilderness, while 'Razzle Dazzle' was taken out of the studio for the first time.

Prior to the show hitting the road, Stephen Bentley-Klein was contacted by a bemused Gillan who complained that the contracted conductor was being difficult, pushing for what would ordinarily be guitar solos to be played on violas and other classical instruments, among other unacceptable demands.

Bentley-Klein's role initially was simply to come in and sort things out. This was a bigger job than expected because not only would the orchestras be different at each gig — he expected that — but another part of the plan was to get local bands to do the rock parts at each venue. As he pointed out, the first part of this was difficult enough.

Trying to do both with only one rehearsal pencilled in for each show was not a recipe for a smooth concert experience. 'Suddenly Don's name came up and he was able to do it,' Bentley-Klein has said. 'And of course, his band contained [the guitarist] Simon McBride.'[10] It could not have been foreseen at the time what a big deal this would prove to be.

Three of the resulting gigs were released, one on vinyl, one on CD (and download) and one on DVD. They are simply astonishing examples of all-round virtuosity. Gillan's generosity as a performer is prominent throughout, as he sits out for long stretches to let the musicians do their thing. Nothing says this more than the presence in the set list of the wholly instrumental — not to mention nothing whatsoever to do with Gillan — 'Difficult to Cure'.

The way everything comes together towards the end of 'No More Cane On The Brazos' is also a brilliant example of the raw emotional power of music. The singer also allowed his daughter, Grace, who was providing backing vocals, to perform a brief duet with him.

According to Bentley-Klein, Gillan was more than a little nervous about this one: 'He said, "does it look bad if I ask her to do something, because I want her to do a song on my set as well."'[11] In fact, the song, 'You're Gonna Ruin Me Baby' is a real — so to speak — grace note in the set.

Of all the different parts that make up the sound, it is the guitar that merits most discussion. McBride's interpretations of the Deep Purple songs were definitely his own. Bentley-Klein's take on this is particularly insightful: 'The thing with rock is that the guitar player almost plays in an aggressive classical manner — a lot of the heavier riffs are very sort of straight, 'I'm just nailing it down'. The drummers like Ian [Paice] and [the Rolling Stones'] Charlie Watts, they all come from essentially a big band background, so when they play it's sort of swingy. Then you've got the guitar player, who plays very straight and aggressive, you know, and that nails the riffs down. That's where the tension, the great tension in rock comes from. Again, it's that thing of these people coming from slightly different areas but forging it together to make it work... To me, Steve [Morse] is more like a sort of — has a bit more of a hippy mentality... he plays a bit more swingy, so I think as the guitar really determines the band — every band is basically the lead singer and the lead guitarist — that's the core... and I think that because Steve plays in a slightly looser way, the band was more expansive, sounds a bit more bluesy — doesn't sound quite so much like nailed down rock… and Simon is much more of a nailed down rock player.'[12]

A good example of this would be their different approaches to 'Perfect Strangers'. On the Montreux recording from the 2011 orchestra tour, Morse lets his guitar howl and whine and blast out feedback. The main riff comes in and drops out, some riffs are rearranged seemingly in the moment.

Meanwhile, Airey keeps everything moving forward, with the orchestra's strings and brass adding the colour. McBride is more disciplined in the Gillan solo gigs. He keeps the riff central and clean and always on the beat. Neither version can fairly be called superior to the other, but they are different. Morse's is more unpredictable, more exciting maybe, McBride's is heavier and more relentless.

In many ways, 2016 was the Year of the Three Axe Men: Blackmore, Morse and McBride. Past, present and, although he did not know it yet, future.

15
The Infinite Goodbye

Despite his not having appeared at the Rock and Roll Hall of Fame induction ceremony, Ritchie Blackmore made a surprising admission in the middle of 2017: 'I think if they would be interested, and our schedules aligned, I would be available for one show [with Deep Purple] — for nostalgic reasons. But I don't think Deep Purple have any interest in that. They have their niche and are not into doing things like that. We are friends and I've been doing my music for twenty years, and they're doing their stuff for twenty years. It's probably not likely [to happen]. Also, their management wouldn't like it, even if it was for just one show. Their management wouldn't allow it, I'm sure.'[1]

Since leaving Deep Purple, Blackmore's life had taken a number of somewhat eccentric turns. Following the hastily recorded Rainbow album *Stranger In Us All*, he had given up on heavy rock, seemingly forever. With the singer Candice Night, he had formed a Renaissance-themed band that went under the see-what-they-did-there name of Blackmore's Night. It should be said that, as far back as his latter days with Purple, Blackmore had spoken of his desire to go in that direction. His relationship with — later, marriage to — Night catalysed his taking the leap.

Together, they released a number of albums with titles such as *Shadow of the Moon*, *Under a Violet Moon* and *Dancer and the Moon*. To be fair, not all of their output was about the moon, but many of the songs' titles had a scent of Disneyesque minstrelsy about them.

The music, though, was not all the kind of twee noodlings that might accompany tales of paladins and fairies. Much of it had a powerful folk-rock edge. The average album included a few covers, with the work of artists such as Jethro Tull, Bob Dylan and Uriah Heep being drawn upon.

Some Rainbow songs were also reworked and live performances featured selections from the Deep Purple catalogue, many of which gained added dimension from being re-arranged for a female voice.

The Rainbow gigs in 2016 and 2017 were supplemental to those of Blackmore's Night and not a substitute for them. In truth, the Rainbow reunion barely deserved the name, being decidedly ad hoc and half-hearted. It produced almost nothing in the way of recorded material — just a few singles, none of which was an original composition — before fizzling out.

As for the gigs, even the most die-hard fan was forced to admit that they were not, on the whole, classics. Blackmore's playing was good, but not at the stellar level of his best days. While the fans were not exactly short-changed, they didn't get a once-in-a-lifetime experience either. One man who was not impressed at all was Joe Lynn Turner. Passed over for the lead singer slot, he was still lambasting the whole enterprise several years later.

Beyond his 'nostalgia' claim, Blackmore gave no reason for his sudden volte face on the notion of playing again with Purple. It would no doubt have been highly profitable, but fan-service and artistic fulfilment were the official line. It hardly mattered. His old adversary Gillan was quick to nix the whole idea: 'Ritchie was a difficult character — there's no denying that,' he said, 'Ritchie and the band got divorced. He walked out in the middle of a tour, and the rain stopped and the sun came out for the band. It was like that. Ian Paice came alive again; he was a happy guy. And Jon Lord regained his gravitas, and Roger came out from under a rock. Everyone started being a normal person again.'²

So that was that. Or, it would have been if talk of Blackmore appearing one more time with the band had not simply refused to go away. As late as 2022, Gillan was still having to say that it would not happen, that it would be disrespectful to the current band, that it would only be for the money. It may never really have been Jon Lord's dream to get everyone back together, but a lot of fans were unwilling to let go of the possibility.

It is ironic that one of the advocates of such a move was Steve Morse, given how many fans still did not accept him as a replacement for Blackmore. Facebook posts and fan forums frequently denied that anything on which he played was a 'proper' Deep Purple album.

None of this treatment was fair, of course — to Blackmore or Morse. But, in an age of Internet-enabled vocal minorities, it was a debate that never completely resolved itself.

Be that as it may, the creative momentum engendered by Bob Ezrin was showing no signs of letting up and a new album was in the works remarkably quickly by Deep Purple's standards. The haste perhaps had much to do with advancing age.

Most of the band's members were now in their seventies; they were beginning to test the boundaries of what might constitute a rock and roller's career. Press kit interviews had the band speculating on whether the new album would be their last. Gillan and Glover were not sure, Airey was emphatic that it would not be. Morse nodded enigmatically. All that seemed clear was that a last album could not now be too far in the future — if this was not it. For Morse, there was the added issue that his constant playing had wreaked havoc on his hands, which were now frequently feeling the pain.

An Ezrin-led period in Nashville produced *Infinite*. The first thing confronting any potential buyer of this was the cover, which was another exercise in slickness. Counterintuitively, this is never that good a sign. *NOW What?!* had gone out under nothing more than a large '?!' against a blank background.

The new album's cover featured a picture of a distant icebreaker that had followed an unusual course, since it had carved out a line that managed to be both the mathematical symbol for infinity and the letters 'dp'. As a cover, it was technically superb, but then, so were the covers for *Abandon* and, going further back, *The House Of Blue Light*, neither of which were musical masterpieces.

Of the music, it can probably be said that this is Deep Purple at their most political and, at the same time, personal. Several tracks are essentially short stories, telling of allegedly true events, some featuring as their main character the younger Gillan. They are pleasant enough, but not standouts.

'On Top Of The World' recounts the tale of a drunken party on the roof of a Far Eastern bank hosted by a group of working girls who lose their allure in the cold light of sobriety; its spoken story-telling section is fun and anticipates a more serious use of the form in the future. 'One Night In Vegas' is similar in concerning a man who wakes up next to an unfamiliar woman who he married the previous night while blind drunk.

Most enjoyable is the one that Paice described as the album's 'pop' song, 'Johnny's Band'. Covering similar ground to 'No One Came' from the *Fireball* album (although in a less cynical way), it follows the rise and fall of a rock band in moving detail.

Gillan stated that it was about the pernicious effect of fashion: to be in fashion one day means, by definition, being out of fashion the next. For him, the moral of the story is that Deep Purple had avoided the fate of Johnny's Band by handily never being in fashion.

The political songs are a little hit and miss. Gillan gave his motivation for writing them: 'I was an angry young man, then I went through a period of complacency in middle age and now

I'm fucking furious!'[3]

He went on to claim that it was 'politics mostly' that caused his anger. Speaking in 2022, Glover took a slightly different line, saying, 'We are an apolitical band and in no way was our intention ever political. It was music.'[4]

In fact, Deep Purple have written plenty of protest songs, but they have always been vague in their targets. Older tracks such as 'No No No' and 'Strangeways' are very much of the 'it's all lousy, but we're not sure what 'it' is' school of lyric writing. Even 'Child In Time' is only anti-nuclear because Gillan says it is.

The band's general attitude to politics is summed up nicely by the *NOW What?!* track 'Hell To Pay' which concerns one 'Two Tone Eddie' who advocates Revolution, despite taking the view that there's 'nothing wrong with the way it was, that's the way it's meant to be'.

Infinite's political posturing begins with the opening track, 'Time For Bedlam', which is probably about being oppressed. Probably. It does include the evocative lyric, 'sucking my milk from the venomous tit of the state'.

'Birds of Prey' talks about war and faith, retreading some of the ground covered by *Rapture Of The Deep's* 'Before Time Began'.

The most effective political track is 'Hip Boots', which rails against slavery. This one had been previewed during gigs in Europe the previous year under the title, 'Got My Hip Boots On'. Poor quality footage of it appearing on YouTube — together with a generally less than ecstatic reaction from fans — led to its being dropped, at least until after it had been perfected in the studio.

The most, as it were, surprising track on the album is 'The Surprising', the apparently incomplete title of which had a noteworthy origin, as Glover explained: 'Steve started playing that opening little guitar pattern and it was something very unusual. And we all started jamming around it and it all felt really lovely to play. Very distinctive from the get-go. The working title was 'The Surprising Mr Morse.' I don't why. The words 'the surprising' don't actually appear in the song anywhere.'[5]

The lyrics, with their talk of devils, angels and the curse of Tutankhamen, are rather opaque, but a good fit for the eerie music. The line about everything going dark 'that August day' can be taken as a reference to Hiroshima.

The longest track on the album, its changes of tone and tempo are somewhat reminiscent of 'Child In Time'. It was given an animated video in which the band is seen sailing around the Arctic on the icebreaker from the album's cover, running into reminders of Deep Purple's past releases. Magnanimously, these include those that do not feature Gillan, Glover, Morse or Airey.

For all that, *Infinite* is not a completely satisfactory piece of work. Playing it from start to finish does not take long, which all concerned seem to have realised, since they tacked on to the end an interminable and unnecessary cover of The Doors' 'Roadhouse Blues': this has got 'filler' written all over it.

Despite 'The Surprising's best efforts, there is also a lack of texture to it all. It is not boring by any means, but the aural variety of *NOW What?!* is only there in spots. Untangling 'One Night In Vegas', 'Get Me Out Of Here' and 'On Top Of The World' in the mind is not easy; one melds into the other even after a lot of listens.

Released on 17th April 2017, *Infinite* repeated the performance of *NOW What?!* by achieving high placings in the charts without actually selling all that many copies. It did particularly well in Finland and Germany. In the latter territory, it hit Number 1 and was awarded Gold certification.

The reviews were generally positive, continuing the Ezrin-era winning streak. Typical was that from *Metal Hammer*, who opined: 'Deep Purple may not have the energy of kids starting out, but why should they? *Infinite*, though, is a graceful, powerful statement that this classic band is still relevant and still making charismatic albums.'[6]

As a title, *Infinite* promises a lack of boundaries and an endlessness that could be temporal, as well as spatial. But the band were careful to avoid making the promise that they would go on forever. Gillan may have been ambivalent about making any more albums, but, in interviews, he was giving the band around another two years. Age was catching up with everyone. Morse's fingers were hurting, while Paice had suffered a minor stroke in 2016 that affected his right hand, leading to the cancellation of several gigs.

The tour in support of the album was called — without irony — The Long Goodbye. It was a bet-hedging title, the emphasis being on 'long' and not 'goodbye'. Gillan commented on this in a later interview: 'Everyone in the band was unwell, we all had health problems, which have been well documented, and I think somebody — and I can't remember who said it, probably somebody from the office — said, "Do you guys wanna call it a day? Because you all have got health problems here." Getting a decision from Deep Purple is always very tricky. So I guess there were a few nods and "hmmmm," "well," "yeah," "maybe," "I don't know…" So we [said], "Let's call it 'The Long Goodbye,'" and that way, we can make our decision later.'[7] Morse was quoted as saying that it would be his "farewell tour."'

It began in May 2017 and took the band on an epic journey around Europe, North America, South America — and other places. The set lists were not liberally peppered with *Infinite* tracks: 'Time For Bedlam' and 'Birds Of Prey' were more-or-less constants, with 'Johnny's Band' being added occasionally.

A notable stop was to headline the annual Hellfest festival in Clisson, France, in June. Recordings from this performance appeared both as a dedicated album release, B-sides to singles and bonus tracks to the inevitable expanded edition of *Infinite*.

No one could say exactly how long the tour would go on for, but it finally came to an end in December 2019. The band returned from it filled with zeal to record a new album. It was not, after all, a goodbye. But it did prove to be a 'see you later' because they — and the rest of the world — were about to be hit by something that would ground them and cause them to rethink many of their plans.

16
Man (Still) Alive

On 16th November 2017, Deep Purple had taken a break from wishing the world a long goodbye to record a live gig for the BBC at the Corporation's Radio Theatre. Not a full concert — it lasted for just over an hour — it was based around one of the band's more interesting set lists. *Infinite* was well represented, with even 'The Surprising' getting an outing. 'Uncommon Man' was included, as were rarely performed oldies such as 'Bloodsucker' and 'Fireball'.

A very competent and enjoyable performance, it has not, at the time of writing, been officially released as an album. This is a pity, since, as a document of the band's situation at the time, it would have — at the very least — historical value.

During breaks in the main touring schedule, Paice was keeping himself busy, playing with jazz bands — London's famous venue Ronnie Scott's being one of his haunts — and taking the drummer's seat with Purpendicular. This does not man the album but a collective who had started their career as a Deep Purple tribute band, before broadening out to write their own material.

It was not the first time that Paice had done this sort of thing. He had performed in a guest capacity with other tribute bands. But this was the first time that he effectively became a full member of a band — to the extent of appearing on recordings. It had come about in the first place as a result of his friendship with Purpendicular member Robby Thomas Walsh. According to Walsh, they had first met in Manchester in 1996 and had taken it from there. As the band's name suggests, the Purple songs covered tended to be from the Morse era.

However, Paice was forced to sit out some Purpendicular gigs in February 2019 because Deep Purple — the actual band — had booked some writing sessions. News of this came out in an unlikely way.

In May, Gillan, Glover and Paice dutifully turned up to Grosvenor House, London, to pick up an Ivor Novello Award for the Mark II line-up's international legacy. Given for achievements in songwriting, it was a belated recognition of Deep Purple's artistry and significance. Gillan was particularly happy with it, stating that his grandfather, an opera singer, would have been 'thrilled to bits' by it.

The grandfather, Gillan said, had been a big fan of the singer-songwriter after whom the award was named. Blackmore's absence this time was uncontroversial — perhaps because the Ivor Novellos are lower key than the Rock and Roll Hall of Fame, perhaps because no one ever seriously expected him to attend.

Speaking on the red carpet, Paice had this to say regarding future plans: 'We've messed around in the studio for a few weeks — we were in Nashville last month. We've got some stuff. We're not making any promises on it. If it turns out to be good enough, we'll do something with it — and if it doesn't we've had five nice weeks in Nashville.'[1]

The mention of Nashville, of course, is the clue that Bob Ezrin was again involved. *Infinite* was not to be the last album after all, nor even the last with the eminent producer. But talk of last albums refused to go away.

Glover addressed the issue during the recording sessions: 'I got asked this when we did *NOW What?!*, which was — what? — eight years ago. Then we did *Infinite*, or 'In-fie-night' and Don was asked, is this the last album, and he said, "I thought the last album was the last album."'[2]

Ezrin appended to these remarks an enigmatic 'maybe, maybe not'. Such coyness is not unreminiscent of the Long Goodbye Tour that actually wasn't, but it does not disguise the clear impression that the album gives of having been planned as the band's farewell.

Exhibit A would be the title, *Whoosh!* Gillan explained it as, 'a kind of onomatopoeic word, and it kind of illustrates the transient nature of humanity on the planet. It's a little subplot. It also describes Deep Purple's career quite nicely. Like over in a second. I mean, 1970 seems like yesterday.'[3]

It is also the final word of one of the album's more notable tracks, as well as the best way to describe the sound that begins the song 'Fireball'. Either way, time is a central idea and not, in this case, abstract time, or objective time, but time as experienced by individuals and not just any individuals. It is time as experienced by the members of Deep Purple.

Another clue is the album's last track, a reworking of 'And The Address', which opened the band's first album, *Shades Of Deep Purple*. In fact, it is not the last track, another song, 'Dancing In My Sleep', appearing after it. That, though, is officially a bonus track, although, since it is in exactly the same place on every release and format of the album, it is difficult to see what kind of a 'bonus' it represents.

Nonetheless, it is clear that 'And The Address' is meant to be taken as the end of the album, thus closing a loop that was opened in 1968. A similar theme is developed on the album's cover. Just the right side of 'too clever by half', it depicts an astronaut on an alien planet disintegrating into dust particles.

Was the potential buyer supposed to see this as a message that whatever was to be found inside would be the band's final graceful fading away? Easy to miss is the band's name (the album's title is absent), which is rendered in a font that is almost identical to that used on 'Shades...'

Still, whether 'last album' or merely 'latest album', *Whoosh!*

is the one that finally lives up to the promise of the Ezrin era — and perhaps of the entire Morse era. Ezrin stated that it was more energetic than its two immediate predecessors and he was right. There really is not a bad track on it. It is more political than *Infinite*, but in the right way. It is less inconsistent than *NOW What?!*, which, for all of its excellence, still includes a couple of rather forgettable songs. It is also more musically adventurous than either: Glover lauded it for going to places that Deep Purple had never been to before.

This is hinted at straightaway, with 'Throw My Bones', which was released as a single some time ahead of the album. An enjoyable mid-tempo rocker, it ironically extols the virtues of not engaging with the world at large. The main riff is backed by some keyboard-supplied strings, giving it a proggy sound. Its best part is the guitar solo, which ups the ante as Airey provides some massive organ chords in the background. It is more than a little breathtaking, although somewhat similar to a passage in Yes's 'Starship Trooper'.

Then again, the accompanying video followed the the album cover's astronaut — a time traveller or extra-terrestrial — as he wandered around a present day city, observing, but not necessarily understanding. Perhaps, then, the Yes reference was intentional.

Next up is the first piece of overt commentary, 'Drop The Weapon', which decries street violence against a fast-paced blues-rock backing track. 'We're All The Same In The Dark' slows things down without losing its heaviness. The lyric is about tolerance, its reference to something unexplained that happened 'down in Mexico' adding mystery.

Track 4, 'Nothing At All' has the singular distinction of having displaced 'Razzle Dazzle' as Gillan's favourite Deep Purple song: 'I was thrilled with that, and I'm still stimulated by that. When I turn it on, it just makes me smile, the sheer… what Steve and Don do on those riffing sections is magnificent. And the way it comes in and then resolves into the modulation and into Don... I mean, what would you call it? That wonderful Bach fugue in the middle. I hope I'm not overselling, but I love it.'[4]

Like 'Throw My Bones', the song is a warning against complacency, chastising people for declaring as 'nothing at all' the danger of the 'old lady' — Mother Nature — turning against them.

'No Need To Shout' is another point-maker. This time the lyrics entreat others to engage in productive dialogue, rather than attempting to silence any with whom they disagree. The organ lead-in is essentially the same as that from the beginning of 'Perfect Strangers'.

It is not the song's only allusion, Airey's piano solo quoting from Gershwin's 'Rhapsody In Blue'. 'Step By Step' is another slow burning heavy track — again given a few baroque keyboard and guitar stylings.

'What The What' is a lighter moment. Lyrically, it is in the same 'let the good times roll' zone as 'Razzle Dazzle'. Musically, it is unadorned rock and roll. Glover described it as being in the same vein as the work of Chuck Berry and Little Richard.

Ezrin particularly enjoyed the title, saying that the more expected 'what the fuck' would be 'cheap', adding, 'It's a great turn of phrase and... people in their heads hear 'what the fuck', but he's saying, 'what the what.''[5]

Ezrin described it as an 'Ianism', a reminder of how adept Gillan has always been at making the English language dance to his tune. 'Long Way Round' is a great piece of heavy rock with a riff that echoes some of those from *In Rock*. Its changes of tempo and dynamics add to its sense of drama.

'The Power Of The Moon' was described by Glover and Ezrin as probably the hardest to write from the backing track. Ezrin praised the 'madrigal' like quality of the chorus, pointing to its Englishness. It is certainly a moody, haunting piece of music.

It might be thought that that would be that. Ten tracks (plus a bonus) adding up to an excellent album with which — possibly — to end a career. But *Whoosh!*'s trump card is still to be played. 'Remission Possible' is an instrumental that begins as a mad dash of unhinged keyboard and barely controlled guitar that, around two thirds of the way through its brief running time slows down to become quietly meditative. But this is only a ruse.

It proves not to be a standalone track, but a prologue. In this sense, it is another callback to Deep Purple's earliest days, when such instrumental introductions were a characteristic of the band's sound (as with 'Prelude: Happiness'/ 'I'm So Glad' on *Shades Of Deep Purple*).

The main track comes in via a segue to a string section (yes, an actual string section) that is just sublime. The strings fill the air with aching melancholy as Gillan sings of a young man's death and his mother's grief. The rock instruments gradually build up until they break out into the albums best riff. The verse is fast-paced and deals with environmental collapse, through the description of a post-human world.

There follows a story-telling section that adds further complexity; the ticking of a clock in the background brings urgency as acoustic and electric instruments struggle to resolve themselves. This happens with Morse's solo, which is suitably apocalyptic. The verse is repeated, followed by a shorter spoken section and the final word, 'whoosh'.

The song is 'Man Alive'. It could be called the song for which 'The Surprising' is a first draft. It should be played to anyone who cares to argue that rock musicians are not 'proper musicians'. It can plausibly be proposed as the masterpiece of the Ezrin era of Deep Purple; arguably, it is the masterpiece of the entire Morse era.

If that iteration of the band ever produced anything better, it is difficult to name it off the top of the head. As a track, its only real fault is that it renders the final two tracks on the album, 'And The Address' and 'Dancing In My Sleep' (the album's pop song and innovative in its own right) anti-climactic by comparison.

Whoosh! was released on 12th June 2020. The ensuing tour — which was organised without reference to the previous one having been called 'The Long Goodbye' — was a triumph, taking in dates in the UK in October of that year.

Ah! But, of course, as any reader is all too aware, neither of those things happened.

At around the time that the first songs from *Whoosh!* were being released as singles, news was coming from China of an outbreak of a novel coronavirus, one that came to be called Covid-19.

At first, it was easy to think of it as distant, irrelevant, someone else's problem. It was restricted to a single region in the Far East, Wuhan, so it was bad for anyone who lived there, but not something for the rest of the human race to lose sleep over, even if it was very infectious and costing lives. For most of the world, business went on as usual.

The Chinese government battled to contain it but reports soon came through of cases in Singapore and India. Then, all of sudden, Italy was affected. Huge swathes of the population were succumbing. There seemed to be no way to control it. France was next. Inevitably, it hopped the Channel.

A new phrase entered the common lexicon, 'social distancing'. The advice of health professionals was that the best way to avoid catching what — for all anyone knew — could have been a fatal dose was simply to stay away from other people. Events that attracted crowds were banned. Football matches. Race meetings. And rock concerts. Deep Purple's tour had not yet got going. There was still a chance that the disease might be beaten in time for it to go ahead as planned.

But the virus continued its unstoppable surge, passing from human body to human body like memes on the Internet. The World Health Organisation declared a pandemic. Panicking governments decided that there was only one way to stop it.

Lockdown.

What has often been termed 'the great lockdown' started in around April 2020 and went on for several months. It involved almost every country in the world (with the notable exception of Sweden) banning its citizens from leaving their homes except under limited and strictly controlled circumstances. The wearing of masks that covered the mouth and nose was mandatory: breathing out potentially harmful germs was to be avoided at all costs.

Future historians may come to view the lockdown as a form of global collective madness. It certainly had a surreal quality to it. Places that were usually the world's busiest became deserted over night. Roads were devoid of cars. Flights were cancelled in their tens of thousands. Shops closed. Bars were shuttered. People cowered behind closed doors. Those that could work from home did so. Those who could not had nothing much to do but sit there and throw their bones. 'Man Alive', the lyrics of which portray a world taken over by animals grazing on 'grass that grows on city streets', came to seem less like science fiction and more like current affairs.

As for the members of Deep Purple, Glover's take was interesting, if predictable: 'In some ways, the Covid lockdown was like a dress rehearsal for our retirement. And as much as we all loved the opportunity to have all this additional time with our families, it's clear that none of us are ready for a life without music and artistic expression just yet. We have so much fun doing this band.'[6]

Gillan took a characteristically pragmatic line, one that occupied similar territory to that of many of his, Glover's and Ezrin's *Whoosh!* lyrics: 'We've got to learn to live with [the pandemic]. I think everyone's heard that said a hundred times. If we didn't meet people because we think they might have a cold or might have the flu or might have some political views that we don't agree with that might infect us, we have to stop living, if we end up like that.'[7]

The release of *Whoosh!* was pushed back to 7th August, by which point it was supposed that the crisis would be over. The tour was postponed. Since the whole tour was affected, everything was rescheduled for the same time the following year. The UK leg, for example, would now take place in October 2021.

Surely, by then, the virus would have burnt itself out, or a vaccine would have been found, or something — anything — would have been done. Surely. Anyway, it was just unimaginable that things would not have returned to how they had always been by then. Unimaginable.

17
Locked Down And Out

On 6th September 2021, the Deep Purple fan community was taken aback by the sudden appearance of a website called TurningToCrime.com. Its only content was a series of black and white photographs of the band's members in the style of police mug shots, next to a countdown clock that would reach zero on 6th October. Speculation as to what it might mean filled forums and fan sites.

What would happen when the timer ran out? The publication of tour dates? Final retirement? The news that Gillan and Co had indeed decided to quit showbiz and set up as a rather venerable outlaw gang? The general consensus leaned towards its being the release of a new album, or, at least, an announcement of the release of a new album. The major clue was the nature of what had every appearance of a marketing campaign: the band had successfully used a similar drip feed approach with *NOW What?!* some eight years previously.

If true — that a new album was coming — it would be surprising in all kinds of ways. For a start, it was still not that long since the appearance of *Whoosh!*. Not since the early seventies had the band been so productive. Moreover, there had been no recording sessions that anyone knew about. How could there be, with lockdowns still disrupting everyone's lives? It was all an enticing mystery.

For its part, *Whoosh!* had been released to strong reviews. The *New Musical Express* called it, 'one of the most stupidly fun and outrageously silly albums of the year — and, goodness, we're all in need of a bit of fun right now, aren't we?'[1]

While not always being quite so flamboyant in their language, other critics broadly echoed these sentiments. Most pointed to the quality of the musicianship, although Airey's boogie-woogie piano on 'What The What' was not always as well-received as it might have been.

A constantly harped upon theme was the band's staying power: that they were still plying their trade over fifty years after their first release (despite only Paice from the current line-up having played on that) was a source of genuine wonder.

The album was a commercial success, too, insofar as that phrase still has any meaning. It reached number one in several countries (including Germany and Finland) and even hit number four in the UK — a lofty position that the band had not occupied for decades. Still, *Whoosh!* has, to date, sold fewer copies than either *NOW What?!* or *Infinite*.

It would be valid — albeit convenient — to blame the pandemic. There is no doubt that it caused an economic downturn from which — at the time of writing — the world is yet to fully recover.

For a while, it looked like the pandemic would never end. As 2021 came around, the virus was still refusing to go away, in defiance of the frequent lockdowns and alarmingly permanent-looking 'mask mandates'. For the band, it became clear that another postponement of the tour was required. Hence, the planned dates were pushed back another year.

This may have had practical benefits, but it meant that, when it finally happened — if it happened — it would be a tour to promote an album that had already been in the market for more than two years. The given reason was the 'health and safety of all our fans, crew and fellow band mates' which were threatened by the 'ongoing difficulties of the COVID-19 virus.'[2]

The band could have sat it out and enjoyed a well-earned break. None of them seem to have done that. Gillan, for one, used the time to get some writing done. He told a Finnish radio presenter that he wrote every day, filling books with notes, essays, stories — anything, it seems, other than songs, which he only ever created 'in the moment' as part of recording sessions.

The others were presumably practising and planning other projects. Whatever that restlessly ticking virtual clock was about, it likely had something to do with whatever had been occupying everyone as they stayed dutifully in their homes, waiting for liberation.

When 6th October arrived and time, so to speak ran out, it was revealed that 'Turning To Crime' was, as had been anticipated, the title of a new album.

Actually, this was not quite the hoped-for surprise, as a track list had already leaked. But that list included titles like, 'Oh Well!', 'The Battle of New Orleans, '7 and 7 Is.' These were already the titles of songs. Was the new album to consist of nothing but covers?

The answer was yes. It was Ezrin — by now, effectively Deep Purple's George Martin — who came up with the idea, taking inspiration from what had become something of a pandemic-specific sub-genre: home recordings by popular musicians.

These were sometimes original pieces, but were often reworkings of existing songs. Some were released on streaming platforms, such as iTunes, others saw the light of day on YouTube. A particularly fun example was the 'Sunday lunch' series produced by King Crimson guitarist Robert Fripp and his wife, eighties pop diva Toyah Wilcox. Based around covers of songs from a wide range of artists — not to mention Ms Wilcox's increasingly tight tops — the explicit aim was to cheer up a world mired in one its glummer epochs.

More ambitious outputs included entire albums recorded under strict social distancing conditions, which came to be seen as a challenge to be overcome. If Deep Purple were to follow Ezrin's suggestion, a covers album would be the default option.

An album of originals was out of the question: how could the band take their usual 'see what comes from a bit of jamming' approach to writing if they were not able to be in the same room at the same time?

To be sure, the proposal did not gain immediate assent from everyone, Gillan telling *Classic Rock* that, 'I was totally against it to start with. I thought that Purple purists, myself among them, would see something like this as criminal, metaphorically speaking, so initially I didn't like the idea at all. And then I started tapping my fingers on the desk at home, and thinking: "Hmmm, well, what are we going to do for the next year if nothing is happening?"'[3]

That Deep Purple are a creative writing band made the decision to go down the covers route a difficult one for a large constituency of fans to accept. But, in many ways, it had already been prepared for, with all of the 'Time Trilogy' albums having included some kind of cover (if only of the band's own older material).

Many singers and bands had also jumped on the covers band wagon in recent years, with everyone from Status Quo to Bryan Ferry to Nobel Literature Laureate Bob Dylan putting out albums on which they performed other people's works.

Central to the success of any covers album is the choice of songs to be included. Deep Purple took their usual democratic approach. As Gillan said, 'The selection process wasn't anything to do with specifically that we liked this kind of music, or this kind of singer, or that kind of approach, or that kind of song, or it had some great memories for us from the past. It was nothing like that. What we did was sling in about fifty ideas and the reason — you know Deep Purple is primarily an instrumental band — so what we were looking for was stuff that we couldn't improve, but that we could Purpleise and by that I mean that gave the guys a chance to stretch out.'[4]

His own suggestions were roundly rejected by the rest of

the band, but he did not take that personally, arguing, plausibly, that the final decisions had to be driven by what the musicians wanted to play.

'Eclectic' could best describe the songs that made the final cut. Some might seem obvious for a hard rock band — Fleetwood Mac's 'Oh Well', Cream's 'White Room', The Yardbirds' 'Shapes Of Things' — but others are distinctly left field — Louis Jordan's 'Let The Good Times Roll', Johnny Horizon's 'The Battle Of New Orleans'. Perhaps the chief fascination of the final list is what it says about how Deep Purple view themselves. The oft-made claim that they do not fit into any specific genre is certainly borne out by the songs that they chose to 'Purpleise'.

The recording process necessarily had little in common with how things had hitherto been done. The musicians recorded their parts at home, with Ezrin as the ringmaster bringing everything together. 'It was a challenge getting the sound,' Glover told *Forbes* magazine. 'But Bob was a mastermind. When he did the mixes, he just made it sound as if we were all in the same room.'[5]

His method was to allocate a few songs to each instrument, which would then lay down a basic backing track to which everyone else — closed off in their Covid-proof cocoons — played along. Gillan was the only member of the band without a home studio (although, as Glover observed, these days a computer is a home studio), so a call from Ezrin secured Gillan some time at Peter Gabriel's place to lay down the vocals.

There were some unexpected advantages to this methodology. Solos could not be improvised in the moment and so had a more considered and arranged quality than would normally be the case. 'The Battle Of New Orleans' was also the vehicle for a certain amount of novelty.

Part of the set for Gillan and Glover's pre-Purple band Episode Six, it had been sung back then by Glover as lead vocalist. On *Turning To Crime*, the opportunity was taken for him to return to that role — at least for one verse. Gillan reported that the inclusion of this song baffled Morse, who could not understand why a predominantly English band wanted to sing about the British getting their asses kicked. He found himself being schooled on the English character, which is largely based around self-deprecation and self-mockery.

Turning To Crime was released on 26th November 2021. The title came from Gillan's flippant answer any time he was asked what he had been doing during the lockdown, saying that he had been 'turning to crime'.

It may also reflect his — and others' — ambivalence about producing a covers album. Was doing so a criminal act? Were the songs not so much covered as stolen? Reviewers generally did not think so, giving the album a thumbs up, albeit a guarded one at times. *Ultimate Classic Rock's* take was that, having accepted both the very idea of a covers album and the choice of songs, the average fan was likely to be pleased with what they heard.[6]

With the passage of a certain amount of time, it can be said that that is to some extent true. The band always maintained that it was all meant to be taken in the spirit of fun. And Deep Purple always sound good when backed by other musicians, such as the horn players, fiddle and squeezebox that add to some of the tracks here. But that is no excuse for too much of the album being made up of songs that are, at best, eccentric picks.

The more 'Deep Purple' style songs — 'Oh Well', 'White Room', Love's '7 And 7 Is' — are just unimaginative inclusions. Does the world really need more covers of these already much-covered songs? 'Shapes Of Things'? Really?

As for the others, most resist all but the most blunt of Purpleisation. Dylan's 'Watching The River Flow' is unwisely turned into quite a heavy rock and roller. 'Let The Good Times Roll' sounds like something from an aging crooner's latest

Vegas residency. 'The Battle Of New Orleans' could be being performed by anyone.

The final 'Caught In The Act' medley, which includes a portion of Led Zeppelin's 'Dazed and Confused' is interesting enough, but rather patchy. It all comes across uncomfortably like the kind of stuff that Johnny's Band might play on Saturday nights at The Crown.

The album did better in the charts than might have been predicted, reaching the top tens of several countries (including, of course, Germany and Finland), but it remains a forgettable interlude. The 'deep' had not only been taken back out of Purple, it had been poked fun at and left crying on a footstep. The bigger concern was whether it would be the band's last album. At the time of writing, it is the latest. There is no guarantee of another. Few fans would think it the best note on which to bow out.

On the plus side, its release coincided with a gradual easing of the conditions that had spawned it. Finally, the *Whoosh!* tour could go ahead. It began with gigs in Florida in February 2022, but, if the band thought that the days of disruption were over, they were tragically wrong.

That they were forced to pull out of a residency on a 'rock cruise' event because of an outbreak of Covid among some of them was only a taster of what was to come.

At around the time that they were picking up their instruments for their first live dates in nearly two years, Russia invaded Ukraine. The initial response from the West was boycotts and sanctions. Companies that had been trading inside Russia for decades pulled out, mostly on a permanent basis. Film releases were cancelled and those involved in the music business rethought their plans. With the city suffering bombardment from the Russian army, the concert that Deep Purple had scheduled for Kyiv on 31st May was called off. The same fate — but for reasons of protest — befell the Moscow concert that was intended for 4th June.

For Deep Purple, the invasion was more than usually significant. This was a band, after all, that had enjoyed close associations with the people who were now — quite literally — calling the shots in the war. The band's members could not be blamed for failing to foresee that such a thing would happen, but some backtracking and humble pie eating was considered necessary.

All of them issued statements. Gillan made no attempt to conceal their friendliness with key figures in the Russian regime: 'If speaking out means we shall never see our Russian friends again, then that is a big sacrifice, but nothing compared with never again seeing our Ukrainian friends who are being killed.'[7]

Morse put the situation into a broader context: 'As a citizen of a deeply divided country, one thing here that everybody agrees on is: Stop this attack on a Country who voluntarily disarmed their nukes to satisfy all the big players. Stop, lower your guns, turn back, help others on the way back!'[8]

Airey, rather priggishly and, no doubt, ineffectually, said that he had written to Dmitry Medvedev to demand the return of an autograph given during the meetings a decade earlier.

The personal, however, was about to overwhelm the political — and, for that matter, the professional — in the lives of the band.

In March, with only a few dates played, Morse announced that he would be taking a leave of absence. It was nothing to do with the doubts about touring that he had been expressing since the early 2000s; it was not to do with the tendon problems that had made playing guitar an increasingly painful occupation for him.

His statement made clear his reasons: 'My dear wife Janine is currently battling cancer. At this point, there are so many possible complications and unknowns, that whatever time we have left in our lives, I simply must be there with her.'[9]

He was emphatic that he was not intending to quit permanently. Speaking to Robert Sas in a radio interview in 2023, he added more detail, 'I always intended to finish with the band doing the last show, and after twenty-eight years, we just had a problem, you know. My wife's cancer advanced to stage four and we just had to be available all the time for whatever needed to happen. I just couldn't go out on a long tour. So that was that. The tour had been booked for, I think, three different seasons — because of Covid, it got cancelled and then booked again, then cancelled again and booked the third time. So, I think it was time to play those shows.'[10]

He ended his original statement by assuring fans that a 'certified world class guitarist' was waiting in the wings to take his place.

The man in question was Simon McBride. Having played with various members of Deep Purple over the years, he was the natural choice. He claimed that he had been considered as a stand-in towards the end of 2021, but Morse felt able to continue. For a while, anyway.

When McBride finally did take up the reins, the chemistry with the others was: 'immediate, to be honest. We had a few days of rehearsal in May, and that's all we needed. And then we did a few shows in Israel, and places like that, which were my first shows, and all we needed were those few days of rehearsal.'[11]

He credited the social, as well as musical, compatibility with the rest of the band as being his chief asset when it came to fitting in; as he said, there are a million guitarists out there and they're all talented. The x-factor often comes down to how well you get on with your colleagues.

With McBride on the road and Morse caring for his sick wife, the sense that an era was coming to an end was inescapable. When, in July, it was confirmed that Morse would not be coming back, it came as no real shock. His statement on that occasion was as open and honest as everything else he had ever said while a member of the band: 'I wish to thank the listeners who so strongly supported live music and turned every show from a dress rehearsal to a thundering, exciting experience. I'll miss everybody in the band and crew but being Janine's helper and advocate has made a real difference at many key points.'[12]

Gillan spoke for the band in saying that above all they would miss Morse's smile. Stephen Bentley-Klein spoke of how sad they all were to be saying goodbye to their colleague of nearly thirty years: 'They're all gentlemen. They all love Steve and no-one wanted him to go.'[13]

He also gave the opinion that McBride brought a youthfulness to the band that was energising and boded well for the future. In September, McBride became the permanent replacement. The Morse era of Deep Purple was officially over.

In summing it up, one word springs most to mind, 'stability'. For just shy of thirty years — an entire generation — the Morse iteration of Deep Purple played together, with the only change being the amicable departure of Jon Lord and the easy assimilation of Don Airey.

McBride's seat at the high table was procured with a similar lack of fuss. It was all a stark contrast to the sturm and drang that had accompanied the latter days of Blackmore's tenure. In part, this was no doubt down to what Gillan has frequently noted to be the ages of the people involved: they were simply too old for a repeat of such shenanigans.

But it can also be attributed to the personality of the guitarist himself. Morse's much-vouched talent speaks for itself, but, on top of that, he seems to be a genuinely nice guy. A good bloke. Generous both artistically and personally, he brought an entirely new sensibility to Deep Purple that kept them together and enjoying their work.

Of that, there is a clear trajectory, even if it is not always one that follows a straight line. In retrospect, *Purpendicular* is the record of a band looking for a new identity. *Abandon* showcases one, but perhaps one that is not authentic to the band as it then was.

The two Bradford misfires should not be dismissed completely because they opened up new possibilities that were belatedly exploited by the 'Time Trilogy'. Ultimately, it is those Bob Ezrin produced works that will stand as Morse's greatest legacy. They could not have been made by the Deep Purple that included Blackmore, or, frankly, Lord. They have a sound that is unique to the particular group of men who did make them, those creative, tenacious, sometimes visionary, sometimes obtuse, but always interesting, always charismatic and, perhaps above all, uncommon men.

Gillan and Paice with The Kerrang! Hall of Fame Award at the Relentless Kerrang Awards at the Troxy in London, 12th June 2014.
(Suzan Moore / Alamy Stock Photo)

Flying colours from Morse at the Nice Jazz Festival on 10th July 2014.
(Tara Photo / Andia / Alamy Stock Photo)

Performing On NBC's Today at Rockefeller Plaza on 23rd July 2015 in New York City.
(Steve Mack / S.D. Mack Pictures / Alamy Stock Photo)

Performing On NBC's Today at Rockefeller Plaza on 23rd July 2015 in New York City.
(John Angelillo / UPI / Alamy Stock Photo)

Don Airey at the NBC Today Show, Rockefeller Plaza, New York, 23rd July 2015.
(Steven Ferdman / Everett Collection / Alamy Stock Photo)

31st Annual Rock And Roll Hall Of Fame Induction Ceremony at Barclays Centre, New York on 8th April 2016. Gillan, Glover and Paice with Lars Ulrich who seems to appear at any mention of Deep Purple. Former members Coverdale and Hughes were also in attendance, but Blackmore chose not to go.
(Dennis Van Tine / UPI / Alamy Stock Photo)

Promoting *Infinite*, Berlin, 21st February 2017.
(Jens Kalaene / dpa-Zentralbild / Alamy Live News / Alamy Stock Photo)

Arena Zagreb, Croatia, 16th May 2017.
(Dario / Alamy Stock Photo)

Roger at the Solid Rock Festival at Allianz Park, São Paulo, Brazil, 13th December 2017.
(Levi Bianco / Brazil Photo Press / Alamy Live News / Alamy Stock Photo)

Paicey and Roger Glover at the Polar Music Prize Award at the Grand Hotel, Stockholm, 14th June 2018.
(Henrik Montgomery / TT News Agency / Alamy Stock Photo)

Morse at the annual American Tours Festival, Tours, France, 14th July 2018.
(Julian Elliott / Alamy Stock Photo)

Receiving the International achievement award during the Annual Ivor Novello Songwriting Awards at Grosvenor House in London, 23rd May 2019.
(Ian West / PA Images / Alamy Stock Photo)

Morse took time off to be with his ill wife and Simon McBride from Don's own band stepped in. He was officially confirmed as Purple's new guitarist in September 2002. A new chapter begins. McBride at The O2 Arena, London 20th October 2022.
(Bart Lenoir / Alamy Stock Photo)

Epilogue:
After Time Ended

The audience is expectant. The lights have just gone down. Holst's 'Mars, The Bringer Of War' is portentously booming through the speakers

The support band, Blue Öyster Cult (who are not exactly nobodies themselves) have recently completed their slot. An exemplary run through of their greatest hits — 'Godzilla', 'ETI', 'Burning For You' — it ended as it was always going to, with 'Don't Fear The Reaper', accompanied by audience shouts of 'More cowbell!'

Roadies have done their re-sets. Now, after a wait of two long years, the ceremony, it might be said, is about to begin.

The date is 25th October 2022. The place is Birmingham, but not this time the NEC Arena. Now the show has moved into the centre of the city, to the National Indoor Arena, or the Utilita Arena as it is currently being labelled. The bars and restaurants that cluster around it have spent the afternoon serving burgers and beers to the many rock fans - of all ages, but mostly towards the upper end of the scale — who have descended for this much-delayed happening.

People who have not connected for a long-time bump into each other (the author and publisher of this book being two), all drawn by the prospect of hearing their rock idols in concert: for the last time? Perhaps. It has, after all, been potentially the last time for at least a decade of tours now.

Electronic tickets checked, merch bought, last visits to the toilet completed, there is nothing left to do but listen. As Mars continues to bring war, the band assemble on the stage. Glover and Paice, take their places in their usual unassuming, professional way. Airey has found his way behind the keyboards almost unnoticed.

Then the new guy. Short haired, dressed in denim. He picks up his guitar, adopts a stance. The intro music fades out, to be replaced by the familiar staccato lead in to 'Highway Star'. McBride hits the big chords as the build-up continues. Then Gillan enters. Dressed in white to match his hair, which has grown back a little from the short style that he has sported in recent years. Then he is in to the song. His voice sounds good, matching the tight, taut hugeness of the music. Stephen Bentley-Klein was right: McBride is nailing down the riff, keeping everyone else on track, propelling the song forward.

Next is *Machine Head's* shuffle, 'Pictures of Home'. Another one smashed out of the park. Then there are two from *Whoosh!* — the only representatives of the album that is the ostensible reason for being here in the first place. 'No Need To Shout' has presumably been chosen because, on an album laced with baroque stylings, it is relatively simple and anthemic. Projector screens at the back of the stage display selected lyrics from it, using a broken, angry font.

'Nothing At All' is an obvious inclusion, the screens showing animations appropriate to the meaning and message of the piece. A pleasing 'Uncommon Man' follows, then it is back to the older songs: 'Lazy', 'When A Blindman Cries', 'Perfect Strangers', 'Space Truckin'' and, it does not need to be said, 'Smoke On The Water'. 'Anya' is a nice touch, insisted upon, probably, by its main Champion, Gillan.

By the time the encores begin with a tremendous 'Hush', it is clear that whatever this mark of Deep Purple needed to prove has been more than proven.

The standard of musicianship is sky high, the singing the best it has been for years. Above all, everyone looks so well. Healthy. Energetic. Apart from the new recruit, these are men well into their seventies, pushing eighty in some cases. Yet, they have no problem getting through the set, holding the stage, communicating with the audience. Gillan's banter is at its witty best, a reference to Mitzi Dupree — a character from an older song — going down particularly well.

The range of material is open to question. Six of the thirteen songs played are from *Machine Head*, with the post-Blackmore era largely ignored. That is understandable.

Memories of the hostility that Morse faced from some quarters upon tentatively trying on his predecessor's hallowed shoes may have led to a deliberate policy of playing it safe to reassure fans that this is still Deep Purple. In any case, UK fans have generally been among the more conservative in terms of what they expect from a live performance.

The main take away is that, if the crowds have turned up in the belief that this might be their last chance to experience the band live, then the band themselves clearly have other ideas. Whether they are still waving that longest goodbye in history, or just getting on with their jobs, they are not prepared to give up on the future quite yet.

Writing sessions for a new studio album have been booked in. Gillan is off on the road with another orchestra. Deep Purple's 2023 tour schedule is beginning to fill up. What it all adds up to is a kind of affirmation — of the band and of their music and of the fans who turn up loyally every time giving their love, showing their belief.

The 'Time Trilogy' begins with the words, 'time it does not matter' and maybe in the end that is true. As old as they are, the members of Deep Purple are not allowing themselves to be beaten by time and isn't that something to celebrate? They have never been the most fashionable of bands. They have never been especially controversial. But, more than most of their peers, they embody and exemplify that human quality of never stopping, never quitting, never saying this is the end. Time will march on, sure. But, so what? It doesn't matter.

Discography

Singles

Sometimes I Feel Like Screaming / Vavoom: Ted The Mechanic
(CDs, 1996)

Aviator (Radio Edit) / Aviator (Original Version) /
Somebody Stole My Guitar
(CDs, 1996)

Black Night / Fireball
(CDs / 12", 1999)

Haunted / Haunted (Mellow Mix)
(CDs, 2003)

All The Time In The World (Radio Mix Edit) / Hell To Pay (Radio Edit) /
Perfect Strangers (Live) / Rapture Of The Deep (Live)
(CDs, 2013)

Hell To Pay (Radio Edit) / All The Time In The World (Radio Mix Edit)
(7", 2013)

Vincent Price / First Sign Of Madness /
The Well-Dressed Guitar / Wrong Man (Live) / Vincent Price (Video)
(CDs, 2013)

Vincent Price / First Sign Of Madness
(7", 2013)

Above And Beyond / Things I Never Said /
Space Truckin' (Live) / Green Onions / Hush (Live)
(CDs, 2013)

Above And Beyond / Space Truckin' (Live In Majano, Italy)
(7", 2013)

Out Of Hand / Apres Vous (Instrumental) /
Lazy (Live At Wacken Open Air 2013) / Hell To Pay (Instrumental)
(10", 2015)

Time For Bedlam   / Paradise Bar /
Uncommon Man (Instrumental Version) / Hip Boots
(CDs / 10", 2017)

All I Got Is You (Album Version) /
Simple Folk (An Solo Guitar Improvisation By Steve Morse) /
Above And Beyond (Previously Unreleased Instrumental Version) /
Time For Bedlam (First Take From The Album Recordings) /
Highway Star (Previously Unreleased Live Version)
(CDs / 10", 2017)

Johnny's Band (Album Version) /
In & Out Jam (Rehearsal Recording By Roger Glover) /
Strange Kind Of Woman (Previously Unreleased Live Version) /
The Mule (Previously Unreleased Live Version)   /
Hell To Pay (Previously Unreleased Live Version)
(CDs, 2017)

Throw My Bones / The Power Of The Moon / Man Alive
(CDs, 2020)

Albums

Purpendicular (1996)
Tracks: Vavoom: Ted The Mechanic / Loosen My Strings / Soon Forgotten / Sometimes I Feel Like Screaming / Cascades: I'm Not Your Lover / The Aviator / Rosa's Cantina / A Castle Full Of Rascals / A Touch Away / Hey Cisco / Somebody Stole My Guitar / The Purpendicular Waltz / *Don't Hold Your Breath //
*Bonus track in Japan and USA.

Live At The Olympia '96 (1997)
Tracks: Fireball / Maybe I'm A Leo / Ted The Mechanic / Pictures Of Home / Black Night / Cascades: I'm Not Your Lover / Sometimes I Feel Like Screaming / Woman From Tokyo / No One Came / The Purpendicular Waltz / Rosa's Cantina / Smoke On The Water / When A Blind Man Cries / Speed King / Perfect Strangers / Hey Cisco / Highway Star //

Abandon (1998)
Tracks: Any Fule Kno That / Almost Human / Don't Make Me Happy / Seventh Heaven / Watching The Sky / Fingers To The Bone / Jack Ruby / She Was   / Whatsername / '69   / Evil Louie / Bludsucker //

Total Abandon - Australia '99 (1999)
Tracks: Ted The Mechanic / Strange Kind Of Woman / Bloodsucker / Pictures Of Home / Almost Human / Woman From Tokyo / Watching The Sky / Fireball / Sometimes I Feel Like Screaming / Steve Morse (Guitar Solo) / Smoke On The Water / Lazy / Perfect Strangers / Speed King / Black Night / Highway Star //

In Concert With The London Symphony Orchestra (1999)
Tracks: Pictured Within / Wait A While / Sitting In A Dream / Love Is All / Via Miami / That's Why God Is Singing The Blues / Take It Off The Top / Wring That Neck   / Pictures Of Home / Concerto For Group And Orchestra – First Movement I   / Second Movement / Third Movement / Ted The Mechanic / Watching The Sky / Sometimes I Feel Like Screaming / Smoke On The Water //

The Bootleg Series 1984 - 2000 (2000)
Tracks: (Purple Sunshine) Fireball / Black Night / The Battle Rages On / Ted The Mechanic / Woman From Tokyo / The Purpendicular Waltz   / When A Blindman Cries / Perfect Strangers / Pictures Of Home - Jon Lord Solo / Knocking At Your Backdoor / Anyone's Daughter / Child In Time / Anya / Lazy - Ian Paice Solo / Speed King / Highway Star / Smoke On The Water   //
(Made In Japan 2000) Woman From Tokyo / Fireball / Into The Fire / Sometimes I Feel Like Screaming / '69 / Smoke On The Water / Fools / Black Night / Watching The Sky / Steve's Solo / Cascades: I'm Not Your Lover / Any Fule Kno That   / Jon's Solo / Perfect Strangers /
When A Blind Man Cries / Speed King / Ian's Solo   / Lazy   / Hush   / Highway Star //

12-disc box set of officially released bootlegs. Discs 1-8 are of the MKII line-up. Discs 9-12 are two bootlegs from the Morse Era: *Purple Sunshine* (Recorded at the Sunrise Theatre, Fort Lauderdale, 4th March 1995) & *Made In Japan 2000* (Recorded at the Festival Hall, Osaka, 4th January 2000.

The Soundboard Series - Australasian Tour 2001 (2001)
Tracks: (Melbourne Rod Laver Arena, 9th March)   Woman From Tokyo / Ted The Mechanic / Mary Long / Lazy / No One Came / Black Night / Sometimes I Feel Like Screaming / '69 / Smoke On The Water / Perfect Strangers / Hey Cisco / When A Blind Man Cries / Fools / Speed King / Hush / Highway Star //
(Wollongong, 13th March 2001) Woman From Tokyo / Ted The Mechanic / Mary Long / Lazy / No One Came / Black Night / Sometimes I Feel Like Screaming / Fools / Perfect Strangers / Hey Cisco / When A Blind Man Cries / Smoke On The Water / Speed King featuring Jimmy Barnes / Hush / Highway Star //
(Newcastle, March 14th 2001) Woman From Tokyo / Ted The Mechanic / Mary Long / Lazy / No One Came / Black Night / Sometimes I Feel Like Screaming / Fools / Perfect Strangers / Hey Cisco / When A Blind Man Cries / Smoke On The Water / Speed King featuring Jimmy Barnes / Hush / Highway Star featuring Ian Moss & Jimmy Barnes //
(HK Coliseum, Hong Kong, 20th March 2001) Woman From Tokyo / Ted The Mechanic / Mary Long / Lazy / No One Came / Black Night / Sometimes I Feel Like Screaming / Fools / Perfect Strangers / Hey Cisco / When A Blind Man Cries / Smoke On The Water / Speed King / Hush / Highway Star //
(Tokyo 24th March 2001) Pictured Within / Sitting In A Dream featuring Ronnie James Dio / Love Is All featuring Ronnie James Dio / Fever Dreams featuring Ronnie James Dio / Rainbow In The Dark featuring Ronnie James Dio / Watching The Sky / Sometimes I Feel Like Screaming / The Well-Dressed Guitar / Wring That Neck / Fools / Perfect Strangers / Concerto For Group & Orchestra / When A Blind Man Cries / Pictures Of Home / Smoke On The Water featuring Ronnie James Dio //

(Tokyo 25th March 2001) *Pictured Within / Sitting In A Dream featuring Ronnie James Dio / Love Is All featuring Ronnie James Dio / Fever Dreams featuring Ronnie James Dio / Rainbow In The Dark featuring Ronnie James Dio / Sometimes I Feel Like Screaming / The Well-Dressed Guitar / Wring That Neck / When A Blind Man Cries / Fools / Perfect Strangers / Concerto For Group & Orchestra / Pictures Of Home / Smoke On The Water featuring Ronnie James Dio //*

12-disc box set.

Live At The Rotterdam Ahoy (2001)
Tracks: Introduction / Pictured Within / Sitting In A Dream featuring Ronnie James Dio / Love Is All featuring Ronnie James Dio / Fever Dreams featuring Ronnie James Dio / Rainbow In The Dark featuring Ronnie James Dio / Wring That Neck / Fools / When A Blind Man Cries / Ted The Mechanic / The Well Dressed Guitar / Pictures Of Home / Sometimes I Feel Like Screaming / Perfect Strangers / Smoke On The Water / Black Night / Highway Star //

Bananas (2003)
Tracks: House Of Pain / Sun Goes Down / Haunted / Razzle Dazzle / Silver Tongue / Walk On / Picture Of Innocence / I Got Your Number / Never A Word / Bananas / Doing It Tonight / Contact Lost //

Live Encounters… (2004)
Tracks: Fireball / Maybe I'm A Leo / Ted The Mechanic / Pictures Of Home / Black Night / Cascades: I'm Not Your Lover / Sometimes I Feel Like Screaming / Woman From Tokyo / No One Came / Rosa's Cantina / Smoke On The Water / When A Blind Man Cries / Speed King / Perfect Strangers / Hey Cisco / Highway Star //

Rapture Of The Deep (2005)
Tracks: Money Talks / Girls Like That / Wrong Man / Rapture Of The Deep / Clearly Quite Absurd / Don't Let Go / Back To Back / Kiss Tomorrow Goodbye / MTV / Junkyard Blues / Before Time Began / *Things I Never Said //
* Bonus track on Japanese release.

Rapture Of The Deep Limited Tour Edition (2006)
Tracks: Money Talks / Girls Like That / Wrong Man / Rapture Of The Deep / Clearly Quite Absurd / Don't Let Go / Back To Back / Kiss Tomorrow Goodbye / MTV / Junkyard Blues / Before Time Began / Clearly Quite Absurd - New Version / Things I Never Said / The Well-Dressed Guitar (Studio Version) / Rapture Of The Deep (Live) / Wrong Man (Live) / Highway Star (Live) / Smoke On The Water (Live) / Perfect Strangers (Live) //

Live At Montreux 1996 (2006)
Tracks: Fireball / Ted The Mechanic / Pictures Of Home / Black Night / Woman From Tokyo / No One Came / When A Blind Man Cries / Hey Cisco / Speed King / Smoke On The Water / Sometimes I Feel Like Screaming / Fools //

Live At Montreux 2006 - They All Came Down To Montreux (2007)
Tracks: Pictures Of Home / Things I Never Said / Strange Kind Of Woman / Rapture Of The Deep / Wrong Man / Kiss Tomorrow Goodbye / When A Blind Man Cries / Lazy / Keyboard Solo / Space Truckin' / Highway Star / Smoke On The Water //

Live At Montreux 2011 (2011)
Tracks: Deep Purple Overture / Highway Star / Hard Lovin' Man / Maybe I'm A Leo / Strange Kind Of Woman / Rapture Of The Deep / Woman From Tokyo / Contact Lost / When A Blind Man Cries / The Well Dressed Guitar / Knocking At Your Back Door / Lazy / No One Came / Don Airey Keyboard Solo / Perfect Strangers / Space Truckin' / Smoke On The Water / Hush / Black Night //

NOW What?! (2013)
Tracks: A Simple Song / Weirdistan / Out Of Hand / Hell To Pay / Bodyline / Above And Beyond / Blood From A Stone / Uncommon Man / Après Vous / All The Time In The World / Vincent Price / It'll Be Me //

The NOW What?! Live Tapes (2013)
Tracks: Strange Kind Of Woman / Hard Lovin' Man / Vincent Price / Contact Lost / All The Time In The World / No One Came / Bodyline / Perfect Strangers / Above And Beyond / Lazy / Black Night / Smoke On The Water //

Celebrating Jon Lord (2014)
Tracks: Uncommon Man / Above and Beyond / Lazy / When A Blind Man Cries / Perfect Strangers / Black Night / Hush //

Deep Purple's set was released on double vinyl. The full show was released in various other audio and visual formats.

Live In Verona (2014)
Tracks: Deep Purple Overture / Highway Star / Hard Lovin' Man / Maybe I'm A Leo / Strange Kind Of Woman / Rapture Of The Deep / Woman From Tokyo / Contact Lost / Steve Morse Solo / When A Blind Man Cries / The Well Dressed Guitar / Knocking At Your Back Door / Lazy / No One Came / Don Airey Solo / Perfect Strangers / Space Truckin' / Smoke On The Water / Hush / Roger Glover Solo / Black Night //

From The Setting Sun… (In Wacken) (2015)
Tracks: Highway Star / Into The Fire / Hard Lovin' Man / Vincent Price / Strange Kind Of Woman / Contact Lost / The Well Dressed Guitar / Hell To Pay / Lazy / Above And Beyond / No One Came / Don Airey's Solo / Perfect Strangers / Space Truckin' / Smoke On The Water / Green Onions – Hush / Black Night //

…To The Rising Sun (In Tokyo) (2015)
Tracks: Après Vous / Into The Fire / Hard Lovin' Man / Strange Kind Of Woman / Vincent Price / Contact Lost / Uncommon Man / The Well Dressed Guitar / The Mule / Above And Beyond / Lazy / Hell To Pay / Don Airey's Solo / Perfect Strangers / Space Truckin' / Smoke On The Water / Green Onions - Hush / Black Night //

Infinite (2017)
Tracks: Time For Bedlam / Hip Boots / All I Got Is You / One Night In Vegas / Get Me Outta Here / The Surprising / Johnny's Band / On Top Of The World / Birds Of Prey / Roadhouse Blues //

The Infinite Live Recordings Vol.1 (2017)
Tracks: Time For Bedlam / Fireball / Bloodsucker / Strange Kind Of Woman / Uncommon Man / The Surprising / Lazy / Birds Of Prey / Hell To Pay / Key Solo / Perfect Strangers / Space Truckin' / Smoke On The Water / Peter Gunn - Hush / Black Night //

The Infinite Live Recordings Vol.1 (2018 Japanese edition)
Tracks: (disc 1) Time For Bedlam / Fireball / Bloodsucker / Strange Kind Of Woman / Uncommon Man / The Surprising / Lazy / Birds Of Prey / Perfect Strangers / Space Truckin' / Smoke On The Water / Peter Gunn / Hush / Black Night // Tracks: (disc 2) Hell To Pay (Live At Hellfest 2017) / Key Solo (Live At Hellfest 2017) / Highway Star (Live In Aalborg 2013) / Strange Kind Of Woman (Live In Gaevle 2013) / The Mule (Live In Gaevle 2013) / Hell To Pay (Live In Gaevle 2013) / Black Night (Live In Milan 2013) / Smoke On The Water (Live In Milan 2013) / Simple Folk / Above And Beyond (Instrumental) / Time For Bedlam (First Take) / In & Out Jam / All I Got Is You (Radio Edit) / Johnny's Band (Radio Edit) //

Live In Rome 2013 (2019)
Tracks: Fireball / Into The Fire / Hard Lovin' Man / Vincent Price / Strange Kind Of Woman / Contact Lost / Guitar Solo / All The Time In The World / The Well Dressed Guitar / The Mule / Bodyline / Lazy / Above And Beyond / No One Came / Key Solo / Perfect Strangers / Space Truckin' / Smoke On The Water / Hush / Bass Solo-Black Night //

Live in Newcastle 2001 (2019)
Tracks: Woman From Tokyo / Ted The Mechanic / Mary Long / Lazy / No One Came / Black Night / Sometimes I Feel Like Screaming / Fools / Perfect Strangers / Hey Cisco / When A Blind Man Cries / Smoke On The Water / Speed King / Good Times / Hush / Highway Star //

Whoosh! (2020)
Tracks: Throw My Bones / Drop The Weapon/ We're All The Same In The Dark / Nothing At All / No Need To Shout / Step By Step / What The What / The Long Way Round/ The Power Of The Moon / Remission Possible / Man Alive / And The Address / Dancing In My Sleep / *Uncommon Man (Live In Rio 2017) / *Knocking At Your Backdoor (Live In Rio 2017) / *Black Night (Live In Rio 2017) / *Roger Glover And Bob Ezrin In Conversation (Filmed At The British Grove, London, In November 2019) / *Deep Purple - Live At Hellfest 2017 (Full Live Show) /
* Double disc multi-media version.

Live In London 2002 (2021)
Tracks: Woman From Tokyo / Ted The Mechanic / Mary Long / Lazy / No One Came The Aviator / The Well Dressed Guitar / Up The Wall / Black Night / Fools / Jon Lord's Key Solo / Perfect Strangers / Steve Morse's Riff Parade / Smoke On The Water / Speed King / Hush //

Live In Wollongong 2001 (2021)
Tracks: Woman From Tokyo / Ted The Mechanic / Mary Long / Lazy / No One Came / Black Night / Sometimes I Feel Like Screaming / Fools / Perfect Strangers / Hey Cisco / When A Blind Man Cries / Smoke On The Water / Speed King / Hush / Highway Star //

Turning To Crime (2021)
Tracks: 7 And 7 Is / Rockin' Pneumonia And The Boogie Woogie Flu / Oh Well / Jenny Take A Ride! / Watching The River Flow / Let The Good Times Roll / Dixie Chicken / Shapes Of Things / The Battle Of New Orleans / Lucifer / White Room / Caught In The Act:- Going Down - Green Onions - Hot 'Lanta - Dazed And Confused - Gimme Some Lovin' //

Bombay Calling (Live In '95) (2022)
Tracks: Maybe I'm A Leo / Black Night / The Battle Rages On / Woman From Tokyo / Purpendicular Waltz / When A Blind Man Cries / Perfect Strangers / Pictures Of Home / Child In Time / Anya / Space Truckin' / Guitar Solo / Lazy / Speed King / Highway Star / Smoke On The Water //

Live In Hong Kong 2001 (2022)
Tracks: Woman From Tokyo / Ted The Mechanic / Mary Long / Lazy / No One Came / Black Night / Sometimes I Feel Like Screaming / Fools / Perfect Strangers / Hey Cisco / When A Blind Man Cries / Smoke On The Water / Speed King / Hush / Highway Star //

Live In Tokyo 2001 (2022)
Tracks: Pictured Within / Sitting In A Dream / Love Is All / Fever Dream / Rainbow In The Dark / Watching The Sky / Sometimes I Feel Like Screaming / The Well Dressed Guitar / Wring That Neck / Fools / Perfect Strangers / Concerto For Group And Orchestra: First Movement / Concerto For Group And Orchestra: Second Movement / Concerto For Group And Orchestra: Third Movement / When A Blind Man Cries / Pictures Of Home / Smoke On The Water //

Compilations

There have been no complete compilations from the material that stretches over the eight studio albums produced between 1996-2021, although some tracks have been released on compilations that combine both the Blackmore and Morse eras:

BMG's *Purplexed* (1998) includes tracks from the three studio albums and one live album that BMG released between 1990-1997, and as such it includes two tracks from *Purpendicular*. Likewise BMG's 3-disc set, *Gold – Greatest Hits* (2009) includes nine tracks from *Purpendicular*.

Warner Bros in the States 4-disc set *Shades 1968-1998* (1999) also includes two tracks, one each from *Purpendicular* and *Abandon*.

A Fire In The Sky (2017), a 3-disc collection covering the band's entire career includes eight tracks from the albums from *Purpendicular* through to *NOW What?!* Also interestingly this is the only career compilation where the chronological running order starts with the most recent songs ('Hell To Pay' and 'Vincent Price' from *NOW What?!* and finishing with 'Mandrake Root' and 'Hush' from *Shades Of Deep Purple*.

The only two compilations of material solely recorded in the Morse era (predominantly live tracks) are as follows:

Limitless (2017)
Tracks: Time For Bedlam / All I Got Is You / All The Time In The World (Radio Mix Version) / First Sign Of Madness / No One Came (Live In Gaevle) / Strange Kind Of Woman (Live In Wacken) / Perfect Strangers (Live In Tokyo) / Black Night (Live In Milan) //

Exclusively released in the UK with April edition, issue 234 of *Classic Rock* magazine.

Classic Songs Live in Concert (2017)
Tracks: Highway Star / Into The Fire / Hard Lovin' Man / Strange Kind of Woman / Lazy / No One Came / Perfect Strangers / Space Truckin' / Smoke on the Water / Green Onions -Hush / Black Night //

Filmography

Total Abandon: Australia '99 (1999)
Bombay Calling - Deep Purple Live In Bombay '95 (2000)
New, Live & Rare - The Video Collection 1984-2000 (2000)
Around the World 1995 – 1999 (2000)
Deep Purple Live at the Royal Albert Hall with the LSO (2000)
Perihelion (2002)
Live Encounters.... (2004)
Over Zurich (2008)
Live At The NEC (2008)
Around The World Live (2008)
Celebrating Jon Lord (2014)
Live In Verona (2014)
Deep Purple Live at Montreux 2011 (2016)
From Here To Infinite - The Movie (2017)
From The Setting Sun (In Wacken)... (2017)
…To The Rising Sun (In Tokyo) (2017)
Locked Up: The Making Of Turning To Crime (2021)

In addition to these full-length videos (most of which are concert performances), promotional videos have been made for the following tracks:

Sometimes I Feel Like Screaming
Bloodsucker
Haunted
Vincent Price
Johnny's Band
All I Got Is You
The Surprising
Nothing At All
Throw My Bones
Man Alive
Oh Well
7 And 7 Is
Rockin' Pneumonia And The Boogie Woogie Flu

Endnotes

Prologue: The Banjo Player Takes A Hike
1. Gillan, I. (2016). *Ian Gillan: The Autobiography of Deep Purple's Lead Singer*. Music Press.
2. Deep Purple — Interview with Jon Lord. Deep Purple Official https://youtu.be/Vr1PumjEt1c [accessed Thursday 1st September 2022].
3. De Riso N. (2015). When Deep Purple Improbably Returned with *Perfect Strangers*. *Ultimate Classic Rock*, https://ultimateclassicrock.com/deep-purple-perfect-strangers/ [accessed Thursday 1st September 2022].
4. Bloom, J. (2008). *Black Knight: Ritchie Blackmore*. Omnibus Press.
5. Barton, G. (2022). "I looked at the cover and puked" — the bizarre story of Black Sabbath's Born Again. *Classic Rock*,
https://www.loudersound.com/features/i-looked-at-the-cover-and-puked-the-bizarre-story-of-black-sabbaths-born-again
[accessed Sunday 4th September 2022].
6. Bloom, J. (2008). *Black Knight: Ritchie Blackmore*. Omnibus Press.
7. De Riso N. (2015). When Deep Purple Improbably Returned with *Perfect Strangers*. *Ultimate Classic Rock*,
https://ultimateclassicrock.com/deep-purple-perfect-strangers/
[accessed Thursday 1st September 2022].
8. Bloom, J. (2008). *Black Knight: Ritchie Blackmore*. Omnibus Press.
9. *The Highway Star* (n.d.). Jon Lord Interview. https://www.thehighwaystar.com/interviews/lord/jl199401xx_1.html [accessed Thursday 1st September 2022].
10. Ritchie Blackmore interviewed by Neil Jeffries September 9th 1995.
11. Scarlett, L. (2021). Ian Gillan recalls early Deep Purple days: 'I used to eat dog biscuits from the local pet shop'. *Classic Rock*, https://www.loudersound.com/news/ian-gillan-recalls-early-deep-purple-days-i-used-to-eat-dog-biscuits-from-the-local-pet-shop [accessed Thursday 1st September 2022].
12. Deep Purple at the NEC in Birmingham, 9th November 1993. Rocking in the Norselands, https://norselandsrock.com/deep-purple-nec-birmingham-1993/ [accessed Wednesday 31st August 2022].
13. Irwin, C. (2021). Joe Satriani Initially Rejected Deep Purple: 'I Was Offended'. *Ultimate Classic Rock*,
https://ultimateclassicrock.com/joe-satriani-rejected-deep-purple/ [accessed Monday 5th September 2022].
14. Thompson, D. (2003). *Smoke of the Water: The Deep Purple Story*. ECW Press.
15. Blabbermout.net (2022). Joe Satriani: Why I Decided Against Joining Deep Purple, https://blabbermouth.net/news/joe-satriani-why-i-decided-against-joining-deep-purple [accessed Monday 5th September 2022].

1 From A Dreg To Royalty
1. Paul Mann interviewed by the author, 9th December 2022.
2. Jarvis, A. (2022). *Sculpting In Rock: Deep Purple 1968-1970*. Wymer Publishing.
3. Deep Purple's Mark 4 Line Up Band Genesis in I'd 1975. Deep Purple Official, https://youtu.be/GIvDHXNHmb8
[accessed Sunday 11th September 2022]
4. Bosso, J. (2022). 'I Was Like a Mad Scientist, Always Refining': Steve Morse Reveals How He Wrote 'Take It Off the Top'. *Guitar World*, https://www.guitarplayer.com/players/i-was-like-a-mad-scientist-always-refining-steve-morse-reveals-how-he-wrote-take-it-off-the-top [accessed Sunday 11th September 2022].
5. Horsely, J. (2022). Legendary producer Ken Scott says Steve Morse is the best guitarist he has ever worked with. *Guitar World*, https://www.guitarworld.com/news/ken-scott-steve-morse-best-guitarist [accessed Monday 12th September 2022].
6. Bruce Dickinson, of Iron Maiden, is another notable example.
7. Bengtsson, D. (n.d.). Early Morse Days. *The Highway Star*, https://www.thehighwaystar.com/specials/earlymorse/tour.html
[accessed Tuesday 13th September 2022].

8. A Chat With Guitar Legend Steve Morse (Deep Purple/Dixie Dregs). Sea of Tranquility, https://youtu.be/vyPCoPjDpWg [accessed Tuesday 13th September 2022].
9. Steve Morse interviewed by Jerry Bloom, 9th December 2004.
10. Prince, P. (2015). Roger Glover on Deep Purple's Unique Performances. *Goldmine Magazine*, https://www.goldminemag.com/articles/roger-glover-explains-deep-purples-unique-concert-skills [accessed Sunday 6th November 2022].
11. Steve Morse Interview — Joining Deep Purple — iGuitar Magazine Issue 9. *Guitar Interactive Magazine*, https://youtu.be/jm7p4zz9Lng [accessed Thursday 15th September 2022].
12. Setist.fm https://www.setlist.fm/setlist/deep-purple/1994/palacio-de-los-deportes-mexico-city-mexico-bd4b902.html [accessed Thursday 15th September 2022].
13. As related by Ian Paice in the TV documentary Classic Albums: Deep Purple — the Making of *Machine Head*. (2002).
14. Steve Morse interviewed by Jerry Bloom, December 9th 2004.
15. Marije Essink (n.d.) Deep Purple acoustic — Jon Lord, Roger Glover and Steve Morse on South African radio 1995 https://youtu.be/v5lmOeR6Wss [accessed Monday 26th September 2022].
16. Deep Purple *Purpendicular* Studio Footage. Look What We Found https://youtu.be/IS-wMUn6163M [accessed Sunday 30th October 2022].
17. Roger Glover and Steve Morse interview with Dennis Karlsson, 8th March 1996, https://www.thehighwaystar.com/interviews/band/dp199603xx.html [accessed Thursday 22nd September 2022].

2 On The Lonely Road
1. Chartmasters.org (n.d.) https://chartmasters.org/2021/08/deep-purple-albums-and-songs-sales/ [accessed Monday 26th September 2022].
2. Roger Glover and Steve Morse interview with Dennis Karlsson, 8th March 1996, https://www.thehighwaystar.com/interviews/band/dp199603xx.html [accessed Tuesday 27th September 2022].
3. ChartMasters. https://chartmasters.org/2021/08/deep-purple-albums-and-songs-sales/ [accessed Sunday 6th November 2022].
4. Deep Purple — Child in Time: Story Behind the Song. Top 2000 a gogo, https://youtu.be/OkveukuxQ3Y [accessed Sunday 6th November 2022].
5. Gillan, I. (2016). *Ian Gillan: The Autobiography of Deep Purple's Lead Singer*. Music Press.
6. Deep Purple — Child in Time: Story Behind the Song. Top 2000 a gogo,
7. Jon Lord interviewed as part of the *Come Hell Or High Water* video release.
8. Ian Paice and Ian Gillan — Talk About Touring and the New Album Now What?! Radio Broadcast April 2013. https://youtu.be/ipA9DIeBXeY [accessed Saturday 29th October 2022].
9. Tours and Performances, https://www.purple.de/dirk/purple/mark9.php [accessed Saturday 29th October 2022].

3 A Band On
1. Lighting Tower Collapses at Deep Purple Concert in Chile 1997. Deep Purple Official, https://youtu.be/JUnBKZnOIEl [accessed Sunday 6th November 2022].
2. Light tower collapses during Deep Purple concert; 44 injured. AP News, https://apnews.com/article/5f6de71b3d760b9f7556956d993e3fa9 [accessed Sunday 6th November 2022].
3. Diaz, J. (1997). A Bad Night in Santiago. *The Highway Star*, https://www.thehighwaystar.com/reviews/samerica/chile.html [accessed Sunday 6th November 2022].
4. Ibid.
5. The 1997 Studio Album — First Report — June 9th 1997. *The Highway Star*, https://www.thehighwaystar.com/members/rg970610.html [accessed Sunday 6th November 2022].
6. Ibid.
7. Jon Lord Pictured Within EPK.

8. Ritchie Blackmore interview with Neil Jeffries 9th September 1995.
9. Ian Gillan Interview (Part 2) — How About Your Songwriting? Rabbit Attack PR https://youtu.be/jIkt6QUpMIA [accessed Saturday 12th November 2022].
10. Steve Morris on *One Eye to Morocco*. *Darker Than Blue*, https://darkerthanblue.wordpress.com/interviews/steve-morris-on-one-eye-to-morocco/ [accessed Saturday 12th November 2022].
11. Ibid.
12. *Gillan's Inn* CD liner notes.
13. Deep Purple *Abandon* audio press kit.
14. Ibid.

4 A Load Of Orchestras

1. Paul Mann interviewed by the author, December 9th 2022.
2. 'Concerto' Talk with Paul Mann. *The Highway Star*, https://www.thehighwaystar.com/news/2012/10/14/concerto-talk-with-paul-mann/ [accessed Monday 14th November 2022].
3. Marco de Goeij discusses reconstructing the lost musical score for Jon Lord's Concerto in 2011. Dr Drew Thompson, https://youtu.be/JvvRqVt6Vqc [accessed Monday 14th November 2022].
4. Ibid.
5. Jon Lord — Talking Culture Interview. Purple Maniac, https://youtu.be/Vvb-lpgnXEw [accessed Thursday 17th November 2022].
6. Marco de Goeij discusses reconstructing the lost musical score for Jon Lord's Concerto in 2011. Dr Drew Thompson, https://youtu.be/JvvRqVt6Vqc [accessed Thursday 17th November 2022].
7. Tours and Performances, https://www.purple.de/dirk/purple/mark9.php [accessed Saturday 19th November 2022].
8. Jon Lord — Talking Culture Interview. Purple Maniac, https://youtu.be/Vvb-lpgnXEw [accessed Thursday 17th November 2022].
9. Marco de Goeij discusses reconstructing the lost musical score for Jon Lord's Concerto in 2011. Dr Drew Thompson, https://youtu.be/JvvRqVt6Vqc [accessed Friday 18th November 2022].
10. Deep Purple's Jon Lord and Ian Paice backstage in 2000 talking to Kuno. *Deep Purple Official*, https://youtu.be/PyuSSLkW8ag [accessed Saturday 19th November 2022].
11. Paul Mann interviewed by the author, 9th December 2022.
12. Ibid.
13. 'Concerto' talk with Paul Mann. *The Highway Star*, https://www.thehighwaystar.com/news/2012/10/14/concerto-talk-with-paul-mann/ [accessed Saturday 19th November 2022].
14. Jon Lord interviewed by Jerry Bloom, 21st November 2007.
15. Paul Mann interviewed by the author, 9th December 2022.
16. Ibid.
17. Ibid.
18. Deep Purple's Jon Lord and Ian Paice backstage in 2000 talking to Kuno. *Deep Purple Official*, https://youtu.be/PyuSSLkW8ag [accessed Saturday 19th November 2022].
19. RAH Album Update. *The Highway Star*, https://www.thehighwaystar.com/news/news09-101999.html [accessed Saturday 19th November 2022].
20. A Life of Their Own: Long Time Gone. *The Highway Star*, https://www.thehighwaystar.com/specials/songs/longtime.html [accessed Sunday 20th November 2022].
21. Paul Mann interviewed by the author, December 9th 2022.
22. 2000 Orchestral Tour News. *Darker Than Blue*, http://www.deep-purple.net/dpasmags/dtb53/dtb53.html [accessed Tuesday 22nd November 2022].
23. Paul Mann interviewed by the author, 9th December 2022.
24. 2000 Orchestral Tour News. *Darker Than Blue*, http://www.deep-purple.net/dpasmags/dtb53/dtb53.html [accessed Tuesday 22nd November 2022].

5 No Sleep 'til The Exit Door

1. Deep Purple Roger Glover complete 2001 interview. Dave Lawrence, https://youtu.be/gf0wsIgaN84 [accessed Saturday 26th November 2022]
2. Tsioulcas, A. (2014). How the Three Tenors sang the hits and changed the game. *Deceptive Cadence*, https://www.npr.org/sections/deceptivecadence/2014/07/16/330751895/how-the-three-tenors-sang-the-hits-and-changed-the-game [accessed Saturday 26th November 2022].
3. Italian tenor Pavarotti has died at age 71, his manager tells the AP. *Wave3.com*, https://www.wave3.com/story/7033852/italian-tenor-pavarotti-has-died-at-age-71-his-manager-tells-the-ap/
[accessed Sunday 27th November 2022].
4. Deep Purple Roger Glover complete 2001 interview. Dave Lawrence, https://youtu.be/gf0wsIgaN84 [accessed Saturday 26th November 2022]
5. Deep Purple AAA — Modena Italy 2001. *Deep Purple Official*, https://youtu.be/fiUxtB-AlIU [accessed Sunday 27th November 2022].
6. Polcaro, R. (2017). Ian Gillan says that Luciano Pavarotti was envious of him singing. *Rock and Roll Garage*, http://rockandrollgarage.com/ian-gillan-says-that-luciano-pavarotti-was-envious-of-him-singing/
[accessed Sunday 27th November 2022].
7. Polcaro, R. (2020). Deep Purple vocalist Ian Gillan talks about crying when Pavarotti died. *Rock and Roll Garage*, http://rockandrollgarage.com/deep-purple-vocalist-ian-gillan-talks-about-crying-when-pavarotti-died/ [accessed Monday 28th November 2022].
8. Deep Purple, news and stuff. *The Highway Star*, https://www.thehighwaystar.com/news/news08-092001.html
[accessed Monday 28th November 2022].
9. Jon Lord leaves Deep Purple, is replaced by Don Airey. *Blabbermouth.net*, https://blabbermouth.net/news/jon-lord-leaves-deep-purple-is-replaced-by-don-airey [accessed Wednesday 30th November 2022].
10. Jon Lord interviewed by Jerry Bloom, 21st November 2007.
11. McIver, J. (2012). Jon Lord obituary. *The Guardian*, Monday 16th July.
12. Paul Mann interviewed by the author, 9th December 2022.
13. Deep Purple's singer says Jon Lord's departure was a 'relief'. *Blabbermouth.net*, https://blabbermouth.net/news/deep-purple-singer-says-jon-lord-s-departure-was-a-relief [accessed Wednesday 30th November 2022].
14. Jon Lord interviewed by Jerry Bloom, 21st November 2007.
15. *The Highway Star*, https://www.thehighwaystar.com/news/news03-042002.html [accessed Wednesday 30th November 2022].
16. Jon Lord discussing his departure from Deep Purple in 2002. *Deep Purple Official*, https://youtu.be/v97QBHQSThU
[accessed Thursday 1st December 2022].
17. Ibid.

6 Going Bananas

1. Greene, A. (2022). Keyboardist Don Airey on his years with Ozzy Osborne, Deep Purple and Black Sabbath. *Rolling Stone*, https://www.rollingstone.com/music/music-features/don-airey-interview-deep-purple-ozzy-osbourne-black-sabbath-1279044/
[accessed Thursday 1st December 2022].
2. Ibid.
3. Don Airey in conversation discussing his he joined Deep Purple. Deep Purple Official, https://youtu.be/S8MOwI5LXmI
[accessed Friday 2nd December 2022].
4. Ibid.
5. Pras, A. & Guastavino, C. (2011). The role of music producers and sound engineers in the current recording context, as perceived by young professionals. *Musicae Scientiae*, 15(1), 73-95.
6. Michael Bradford Interview (2003) — Deep Purple — The Making of *Bananas*. *Trinkelbonker*, https://trinkelbonker.wordpress.com/2020/03/02/michael-bradford-interview-2003-deep-purple-the-making-of-bananas/
[accessed Sunday 4th December 2022].
7. Steve Morse interviewed by Jerry Bloom, 9th December 2004.

8. Michael Bradford Interview (2003) — Deep Purple — The Making of *Bananas*. *Trinkelbonker*, https://trinkelbonker.wordpress.com/2020/03/02/michael-bradford-interview-2003-deep-purple-the-making-of-bananas/ [accessed Sunday 4th December 2022].
9. Steve Morse interviewed by Jerry Bloom, 9th December 2004.
10. *The Highway Star*. Roger's Final Studio Report, https://www.thehighwaystar.com/news/news01-022003.html [accessed Monday 5th December 2022].
11. Deep Purple's Electronic Press Kit (EPK) for the album *Bananas*. Deep Purple Official, https://youtu.be/Gla0-Oqw6A0 [accessed Sunday 4th December 2022].
12. Michael Bradford Interview (2003) — Deep Purple — The Making of *Bananas*. *Trinkelbonker*, https://trinkelbonker.wordpress.com/2020/03/02/michael-bradford-interview-2003-deep-purple-the-making-of-bananas/ [accessed Sunday 4th December 2022].
13. Ibid.

7 Enraptured

1. Deep Purple's Roger Glover has 'made great progress' on his autobiography. *Blabbermouth*, https://blabbermouth.net/news/deep-purples-roger-glover-has-made-great-progress-on-his-autobiography [accessed Tuesday 6th December 2022].
2. Steve Morse interviewed by Jerry Bloom, 9th December 2004.
3. Ian Gillan interview with Jon Kirkman, March 2006. *Deep-purple.net*, http://www.deep-purple.net/review-files/gillans-inn/gillans-inntreview.htm [accessed Wednesday 7th December 2022].
4. Letter From Ian Gillan. *The Highway Star*, https://www.thehighwaystar.com/news/news03-042005.html [accessed Tuesday 13th December 2022].
5. Deep-Purple.net, http://www.deep-purple.net/review-files/rapture/rapture-epk.htm [accessed Thursday 15th December 2022].
6. Don Airey Comes Home. *The Highway Star*, https://www.thehighwaystar.com/news/news05-062005.html [accessed Thursday 15th December 2022].
7. Deep Purple Rapture of the Deep Official EPK. earMUSIC, https://youtu.be/cU-jJsniDGk [accessed Thursday 15th December 2022].
8. Ibid.
9. Deep Purple — interview (Live 8, Canada 2005). Ivor's Deep Purple Universe, https://youtu.be/aZyWP3ntkGw [accessed Thursday 15th December 2022].
10. Deep Purple Rapture of the Deep Official EPK. earMUSIC, https://youtu.be/cU-jJsniDGk [accessed Thursday 15th December 2022].
11. Deep-Purple.net, http://www.deep-purple.net/review-files/rapture/rapture-epk.htm [accessed Thursday 15th December 2022].
12. Ibid.
13. Deep Purple Rapture of the Deep Review. *BBC Music*, https://www.bbc.co.uk/music/reviews/wnjw/ [accessed Thursday 15th December 2022].

8 To Russia With Rock

1. No Reunion in Montreux. *The Highway Star*, https://www.thehighwaystar.com/news/2006/06/14/no-reunion-in-montreux/ [accessed Friday 16th December 2022].
2. Jon Lord interviewed by Jerry Bloom, 21st November 2007.
3. Baym, N. (2018). Playing to the Crowd: Musicians, Audiences and the Intimate Work of Connection. *NYU Press*.
4. Hensley, K. (2007). *Blood on the Highway: When Too Many Dreams Come True — The Ken Hensley Story*. Grosser & Stein.
5. Deep Purple to Perform Classic Machine Album on Upcoming UK Tour. *Bravewords*, https://bravewords.com/news/deep-purple-to-perform-classic-machine-head-album-on-upcoming-uk-tour [accessed Sunday 18th December 2022].
6. Vincentelli, E. (2006). If You Won't Play the Album, They'll Sing It, From the Top. *The New York Times*, 31st December.

7. Hensley, K. (2007). *Blood on the Highway: When Too Many Dreams Come True — The Ken Hensley Story*. Grosser & Stein.
8. Blincoe, N. (2008). Medvedev Rocks Russia. *The Guardian*, 4th March 2008.
9. Russia's likely next president met with Deep Purple. Kyiv Post, 12th February 2008.
10. Ibid.
11. Loosen Up Your Ties. *The Highway Star*, https://www.thehighwaystar.com/news/2008/02/17/loosen-up-your-ties/ [accessed Sunday 18th December 2022].
12. Medvedev hosts his idols Deep Purple. Reuters, https://www.reuters.com/article/us-russia-medvedev-purple-idUSTRE72M61R20110323 [accessed Monday 19th December 2022].
13. Deep Purple Rapture of the Deep Official EPK. earMUSIC, https://youtu.be/cU-jJsniDGk [accessed Thursday 15th December 2022].

9 One Eye To The Desert
1. Steve Morse interviewed by Jerry Bloom, 9th December 2004.
2. Ibid.
3. Behr, A. (2018). The album at 70: A format in decline? *The Conversation*, https://theconversation.com/the-album-at-70-a-format-in-decline-99581 [accessed Monday 19th December 2022].
4. Krueger, A. (2005). The economics of real superstars: The market for rock concerts in the material world. Journal of Labour Economics, 23(1), 1-30.
5. Johansson, O. & Bell, T. L. (2014). Touring circuits and the geography of rock music performance. *Popular Music & Society*, 37(3), 313-337.
6. Steve Morse interviewed by Jerry Bloom, 9th December 2004.
7. Deep Purple Release Pulled. *The Los Angeles Times*, 28th February 2007.
8. Gillan Unhappy with BMG. *The Highway Star*, https://www.thehighwaystar.com/news/2007/02/27/gillan-unhappy-with-bmg/ [accessed Tuesday 20th December 2022].
9. Deep Purple Release Pulled. *The Los Angeles Times*, 28th February 2007.
10. Ian Gillan explains *One Eye to Morocco*. Noisecreep, https://noisecreep.com/ian-gillan-explains-one-eye-to-morocco/ [accessed Tuesday 20th December 2022].
11. Steve Morris on *One Eye to Morocco*. Darker Than Blue, https://darkerthanblue.wordpress.com/interviews/steve-morris-on-one-eye-to-morocco/ [accessed Tuesday 20th December 2022].
12. Ian Gillan (Deep Purple) *One Eye To Morocco* Official Trailer EPK. earMUSIC, https://youtu.be/Ed63VJCZKuk [accessed Monday 26th December 2022].

10 Strings Attached
1. Steve Morse in *The Birmingham Post*. *The Highway Star*, https://www.thehighwaystar.com/news/2009/09/28/steve-morse-in-birmingham-post/ [accessed Tuesday 27th December 2022].
2. Erickson, A. (2011). Deep Purple's Steve Morse: 2011 Symphonic Tour 'Isn't Going To Be Orchestra-Based'. *Ultimate Classic Rock*, https://ultimateclassicrock.com/deep-purple-2011-orchestra-tour-steve-morse-interview/ [accessed Tuesday 27th December 2022].
3. Ibid.
4. Ian Gillan Interviewed by *The Express and Star*. *The Highway Star*, https://www.thehighwaystar.com/news/2011/10/26/i-haven't-ever-had-any-ambition-in-my-life-i-just-drift-from-day-to-day-with-a-stupid-grin-on-my-face-it's-very-fulfilling/ [accessed Tuesday 27th December 2022].
5. Stephen Bentley-Klein interviewed by the author, 29th December 2022.
6. Ibid.
7. Ibid.
8. Ibid.
9. Ibid.
10. Ibid.
11. Ibid.
12. Erickson, A. (2011). Deep Purple's Steve Morse: 2011 Symphonic Tour 'Isn't Going To Be Orchestra-Based'. *Ultimate Classic Rock*, https://ultimateclassicrock.com/deep-purple-2011-orchestra-tour-steve-morse-interview/ [accessed Tuesday 27th December 2022].
13. Stephen Bentley-Klein interviewed by the author, 29th December 2022.
14. Ibid.

15. Interview with Ian Gillan. *WikiMetal*, https://www.wikimetal.com.br/interview-with-ian-gillan/ [accessed Wednesday 28th December 2022].
16. Ibid.
17. 'Ambassador of Hope' Ian Gillan Recognised 'Friend of Armenians 2014'. Media Max, https://mediamax.am/en/news/society/10117/ [accessed Wednesday 28th December 2022].

11 How Can I See When The Light Has Gone Out?
1. Jon Lord interviewed by Jerry Bloom, 21st November 2007.
2. Ibid.
3. Marlow, L. (2020). Jon Lord: The Last Interview. *Classic Rock*, https://www.loudersound.com/features/archive-jon-lord-s-last-stand [accessed Thursday 29th December 2022].
4. Ibid.
5. Jon Lord — Former Deep Purple Keyboardist Issues Thanks For Support in Fight Against Cancer. *Bravewords*, https://bravewords.com/news/jon-lord-former-deep-purple-keyboardist-issues-thanks-for-support-in-fight-against-cancer [accessed Saturday 31st December 2022].
6. Paul Mann interviewed by the author, 9th December 2022.
7. Ibid.
8. Ibid.
9. Ibid.
10. Marlow, L. (2020). Jon Lord: The Last Interview. *Classic Rock*, https://www.loudersound.com/features/archive-jon-lord-s-last-stand [accessed Thursday 29th December 2022].
11. Sisario, B. (2012). Jon Lord, Keyboardist with Deep Purple, Dies at 71. *The New York Times*, 16th July 2012.

12 What Now?!
1. Stars Pay Tribute to Deep Purple's Jon Lord, BBC News, 17th July 2012, https://www.bbc.co.uk/news/entertainment-arts-18867699 [accessed Sunday 1st January 2023].
2. Whittaker, S. (2012). Deep Purple Colleagues Fondly Remember Jon Lord. *Ultimate Classic Rock*, https://ultimateclassicrock.com/deep-purple-colleagues-fondly-remember-jon-lord/ [accessed Sunday 1st January 2023].
3. Ritchie Blackmore reportedly refused Hughes, Coverdale and Lord Deep Purple reunion. *Ultimate Classic Rock*, https://ultimateclassicrock.com/ritchie-blackmore-hughes-coverdale-lord-deep-purple-reunion/ [accessed Tuesday 3rd January 2023].
4. Producer Bob Ezrin helps Deep Purple channel its past with *NOW What?!* Goldmine, https://www.goldminemag.com/articles/deep-purple-channels-past-help-producer-bob-ezrin [accessed Tuesday 3rd January 2023].
5. Roger Glover and Bob Ezrin in Conversation. Purple Maniac, https://youtu.be/vUmNFt5FTMI [accessed Tuesday 3rd January 2023].
6. Producer Bob Ezrin helps Deep Purple channel its past with *NOW What?!* Goldmine, https://www.goldminemag.com/articles/deep-purple-channels-past-help-producer-bob-ezrin [accessed Tuesday 3rd January 2023].
7. Anastasia Kuvaldina and Andrew Gusenkov interview with Ian Gillan and Ian Paice for Rock FM. *The Highway Star*, https://www.thehighwaystar.com/thsblog/2013/05/16/rocknroll-at-1-oclock-in-the-afternoon/ [accessed Wednesday 4th January 2023].
8. Ibid.
9. Deep Purple — the production of Now What?! Part 1 — Bob Ezrin. earMUSIC, https://youtu.be/f_dNWe5iPxo [accessed Wednesday 4th January 2023].
10. Anastasia Kuvaldina and Andrew Gusenkov interview with Ian Gillan and Ian Paice for Rock FM. *The Highway Star*, https://www.thehighwaystar.com/thsblog/2013/05/16/rocknroll-at-1-oclock-in-the-afternoon/ [accessed Wednesday 4th January 2023].
11. Exclusive interview with Ian Gillan of Deep Purple *NOW What?! Classic Rock Here and Now*, https://www.classicrockhereandnow.com/2013/05/exclusive-interview-with-ian-gillan-of.html [accessed Wednesday 4th January 2023].
12. Anastasia Kuvaldina and Andrew Gusenkov interview with Ian Gillan and Ian Paice for Rock FM. *The Highway Star*, https://www.thehighwaystar.com/thsblog/2013/05/16/rocknroll-at-1-oclock-in-the-afternoon/ [accessed Wednesday 4th January 2023].

13. Deep Purple *NOW What?!* Album Review. Ultimate Classic Rock, https://ultimateclassicrock.com/deep-purple-now-what/ [accessed Friday 6th January 2023].

13 Sunflowers & Jam
1. Stephen Bentley-Klein interviewed by the author, December 29th 2022.
2. Barton, G. (2014). Interview: Ian Paice on the Jon Lord tribute show. *Classic Rock*.
3. Paul Mann interviewed by the author, December 9th 2022.
4. Barton, G. (2014). Interview: Ian Paice on the Jon Lord tribute show. *Classic Rock*.
5. Ibid.
6. Paul Mann interviewed by the author, 9th December 2022.
7. Ibid.
8. Ritchie Blackmore demands Deep Purple payments. *The Guardian*, 13th July 2015.
9. The 'Deep Purple Scheme' Ritchie Blackmore accidentally uncovered. *Rock Celebrities*, https://rockcelebrities.net/the-deep-purple-scheme-ritchie-blackmore-accidentally-uncovered/ [accessed Sunday 8th January 2023].
10. Keay, L. (2019). Finance Boss, 71, who stole 2.4 million form the companies which held the royalties to Deep Purple's back catalogues is jailed for six years. *Mail Online*, https://www.dailymail.co.uk/news/article-6982359/Director-stole-2-4m-companies-Deep-Purple-s-catalogue.html [accessed Sunday 8th January 2023].
11. Ibid.

14 Inducted
1. Deep Purple's Ian Gillan on the Rock and Roll Hall of Fame: 'These are the same people that decided The Monkees were America's answer to The Beatles' Noise creep, https://noisecreep.com/deep-purple-rock-and-roll-hall-of-fame/ [accessed Sunday 22nd January 2023].
2. Micheals, S. (2014). Roger Glover: Deep Purple ambivalent over Hall of Fame call-up. *The Guardian*, 4th September 2014.
3. Original Deep Purple bassist Nick Simper shrugs off Rock and Roll Hall of Fame snub. *Blabbermouth.net*, https://blabbermouth.net/news/original-deep-purple-bassist-nick-simper-shrugs-off-rock-and-roll-hall-of-fame-snub [accessed Monday 23rd January 2023].
4. Jarvis, A. (2017). *Chasing Shadows: The Search for Rod Evans*. Wymer Publishing.
5. Greene, A. (2016). Deep Purple guitarist Ritchie Blackmore won't attend Hall of Fame ceremony. *Rolling Stone*, 19th February 2016.
6. Ibid.
7. David Coverdale says Deep Purple 'prevented' Ritchie Blackmore's Rock Hall attendance. *Ultimate Classic Rock*, https://ultimateclassicrock.com/david-coverdale-deep-purple-ritchie-blackmore-rock-hall/ [accessed Tuesday 24th January 2023].
8. David Coverdale's reaction to Deep Purple preventing Ritchie Blackmore from joining Rock Hall induction. *Rock Celebrities*, https://rockcelebrities.net/david-coverdales-reaction-to-deep-purple-preventing-ritchie-blackmore-from-joining-rock-hall-induction/ [accessed Tuesday 24th January 2023].
9. Ian Gillan says Deep Purple reunion with Ritchie Blackmore's 'would be no fun at all', blasts David Coverdale's 'opportunistic remarks'. *Blabbermouth.net*, https://blabbermouth.net/news/ian-gillan-says-deep-purple-reunion-with-ritchie-blackmore-would-be-no-fun-at-all-blasts-david-coverdales-opportunistic-remarks [accessed Tuesday 24th January 2023].
10. Stephen Bentley-Klein interviewed by the author, 29th December 2022.
11. Ibid.
12. Ibid.

15 The Infinite Goodbye
1. Ritchie Blackmore would reunite with Deep Purple for final concert 'for nostalgic reasons'. *uDiscover Music*, https://www.udiscovermusic.com/news/ritchie-blackmore-deep-purple-nostalgic/ [accessed Thursday 26th January 2023].
2. Ian Gillan explains why a Deep Purple reunion with Ritchie Blackmore won't happen. Ultimate Classic Rock, https://ultimateclassicrock.com/ian-gillan-deep-purple-ritchie-blackmore-reunion/ [accessed Thursday 26th January 2023].

Other titles by the Author

Chasing Shadows - The Search For Rod Evans
978-1-908724-65-6 (2017)

Sculpting In Rock: Deep Purple 1968-70
978-1-915246-06-6 (2022)

Other Deep Purple related titles available from Wymer Publishing:

A Hart Life (Colin Hart with Dick Allix)
978-1-908724-04-5 (2012)

Deep Purple: A Matter Of Fact (Jerry Bloom)
978-1-908724-06-9 (2015)

Deep Purple - The Road of Golden Dust (Jerry Bloom)
978-1-908724-23-6 (2015)

The Deep Purple Family - Year by Year Vol 1 (-1979) (Martin Popoff)
978-1-908724-42-7 (2016)

The Deep Purple Family - Year by Year Vol 2 (1980-2011) (Martin Popoff)
978-1-908724-87-8 (2018)

Nasty Piece Of Work (Jerry Bloom)
978-1-912782-24-6 (2019)

Sensitive To Light: The Rainbow Story (Martin Popoff)
978-1-912782-40-6 (2020)

Deep Purple Stormbringer: In-depth (Laura Shenton)
978-1-912782-60-4 (2021)

Deep Purple Fireball: In-depth (Laura Shenton)
978-1-912782-82-6 (2021)

Deep Purple Slaves And Masters: In-depth (Laura Shenton)
978-1-912782-83-3 (2021)

Rainbow Straight Between The Eyes: In-depth (Laura Shenton)
978-1-912782-96-3 (2022)

David Coverdale: A Life In Vision (Andy Francis)
978-1-915246-00-4 (2022)

Jon Lord: A Visual Biography (Jerry Bloom)
978-1-915246-12-7 (2022)

Ian Gillan A Visual Biography (Andy Francis)
978-1-915246-21-9 (2023)

Perfect Strangers? Deep Purple 1984-1993 (Laura Shenton)
978-1-915246-28-8 (2023)

Rainbow A Visual Biography (Jerry Bloom)
978-1-915246-22-6 (2023)

Ritchie Blackmore A Life In Vision (Jerry Bloom)
978-1-915246-30-1 (2023)

3. Deep Purple's Ian Gillan: 'It's good to get worked up because then you can get some venom into your work'. *Sentinel Daily*, https://sentineldaily.com.au/deep-purples-ian-gillan/ [accessed Saturday 28th January 2023].
4. Deep Purple is apolitical, but... *The Highway Star*, https://www.thehighwaystar.com/news/2022/03/05/deep-purple-is-apolitical-but/ [accessed Saturday 28th January 2023].
5. Deep Purple *Infinite* track by track — 'The Surprising'. earMUSIC, https://youtu.be/9WTfDLZ-Pwjl [accessed Saturday 28th January 2023].
6. Dome, M. (2017). Deep Purple — *Infinite* Album Review. *Metal Hammer*, 24th June 2017.
7. Why Deep Purple named their tour 'The Long Goodbye'. *Ultimate Classic Rock*, https://ultimateclassicrock.com/deep-purple-long-goodbye-tour-2/ [accessed Sunday 29th January 2023].

16 Man (Still) Alive

1. We'll be back in 300 years. *The Highway Star*, https://www.thehighwaystar.com/news/2019/05/28/well-be-back-in-300-years/ [accessed Sunday 29th January 2023].
2. Roger Glover & Bob Ezrin in conversation. Purple Maniac, https://youtu.be/vUmNFt5FTMI [accessed Tuesday 31st January 2023].
3. Popoff, M. (2020). Deep Purple go space trekkin' with *Whoosh!* LP. Goldmine, https://www.goldminemag.com/interviews/deep-purple-go-space-trekkin-with-whoosh-lp [accessed Tuesday 31st January 2023].
4. Ibid.
5. Roger Glover & Bob Ezrin in conversation. Purple Maniac, https://youtu.be/vUmNFt5FTMI [accessed Tuesday 31st January 2023].
6. Deep Purple's lockdown was a 'dress rehearsal for retirement'. *Ultimate Classic Rock*, https://ultimateclassicrock.com/deep-purple-retirement/ [accessed Wednesday 1st February 2023].
7. Deep Purple's Ian Gillan believes that the pandemic is 'finished now': 'I think it will just fade away this winter'. *Blabbermouth.net*, https://blabbermouth.net/news/deep-purples-ian-gillan-believes-the-pandemic-is-finished-now-i-think-it-will-just-fade-away-this-winter [accessed Wednesday 1st February 2023].

17 Locked Down And Out

1. Cooper, L. (2020). Deep Purple — *Whoosh!* Review: rockers' 21st record is stupidly fun and outrageously silly. *New Musical Express*, 6th August 2020.
2. Deep Purple reschedule UK tour for October 2022. *Planet Rock*, https://planetradio.co.uk/planet-rock/news/rock-news/deep-purple-whoosh-uk-tour/ [accessed Thursday 2nd February 2023].
3. Brannigan, P. (2021). How Deep Purple turned to crime. *Classic Rock*, 21st December 2021.
4. Exclusive: Ian Gillan discussing about the future of Deep Purple + new album *Turning To Crime*. Chaoszine, https://youtu.be/q5knD-24YV4 [accessed Saturday 4th February 2023].
5. Ryan, J. (2021). Roger Glover on new Deep Purple album, *Turning To Crime*. Forbes, November 26th.
6. Graff, G. (2021). Deep Purple, *Turning To Crime*: Album Review. 23rd November 2021.
7. Deep Purple is apolitical, but... *The Highway Star*, https://www.thehighwaystar.com/news/2022/03/05/deep-purple-is-apolitical-but/ [accessed Saturday 4th February 2023].
8. Ibid.
9. Steve is taking a hiatus... *The Highway Star*, https://www.thehighwaystar.com/news/2022/03/31/steve-is-taking-a-hiatus/ [accessed Saturday 4th February 2023].
10. Steve Morse interviewed by Robert Sas, February 2023.
11. An interview with Simon McBride of Deep Purple. VW Music, https://vwmusicrocks.com/an-interview-with-simon-mcbride-of-deep-purple/ [accessed Saturday 4th February 2023].
12. Skinner, T. (2022). Deep Purple guitarist Steve Morse officially quits band to care for his ill wife. *New Musical Express*, 23rd July.
13. Stephen Bentley-Klein interviewed by the author, 29th December 2022.